Table of Contents

a reason to live!

a reason to die!

A NEW LOOK AT FAITH IN GOD

JOHN POWELL S.J.

This book is gratefully dedicated
To My Mother.
It has been mainly through her own deep faith,
quiet example, and loving prayers
that God has channeled
his graces of faith to me.
Thanks so much, Jennie.

Introduction

The question:

Have you ever wondered, as most of us have, if you really believe in God, religion, and the reality of Church?

For many of us, when the question of faith surfaced, at some crisis point in life, it was painful and disconcerting, sometimes weighing heavily within the stomach like undigested food.

Maybe for you it came at a time when your back was against the wall, and you wondered about resorting to prayer, when the words of prayer stuck in your throat, and your mind questioned whether prayer is something real or only a shallow superstition.

It may have been on a Sunday morning, when the bells of the nearby Church were summoning the faithful to praise and petition God, and you turned over uneasily in your bed before going back to sleep.

Or when you were planning your marriage, and you found yourself trying to decide between a candle-lit Church and the offices of the local Justice of the Peace.

Or it could have been when someone you had known and loved "passed away," and the thought struck like thunder: What happens after death?

"Do I really believe in God?" You heard the question and it would not sleep.

In search of an answer

Disraeli once said that men are determined in their beliefs by what is "in fashion." The contagion of fashion and environment is too real to deny. There is some strange sense of safety and refuge in the "majority opinion," the "in-thing."

You may have seen the movie, *Charly*. At the height of his surgically induced genius, Charly Gordon said that religion is determined by "popularity polls." Of youth he said "joyless and guideless," and you thought he was talking about a large part of you .

But there is no consolation in the numbers game. The street is dead-end. There are many brainy people, people of impressive intelligence and integrity who have decided this question differently. They are all respectable people with respectable opinions, ranging from hard line atheism to bedrock belief.

Pressures and prejudice

Prejudice is everywhere. There is no shining Camelot that banishes all prejudice or precludes psychological programming. Most human decisions are made in the glands, not by the brain. You know it. I know it.

But something in us wants to shed prejudice, programming, brainwashing. We hate the umbilical cords that shackle us to our past, destroying our

8

freedom of choice. We do not want God, with his candles, incense, and stained-glass windows, just because we have been "brought up" that way.

Religion and patriotism are special areas of suspicion. They seem to promote "convenient" truths, the kind that prejudice plays upon, the kind that comfort men in need and control men in conduct. We are suspicious. We feel manipulated. We don't want to believe because someone else wants us to. That would be only capitulation, an abdication of intelligence.

But not all the tyrants that enslave are outside us. The parasites of human insecurity have invaded all of us, little termites of terror telling us that it is safer to believe, offering a blanket for Linus. God—if he is really there—is not an aspirin, whatever else he may be.

Prejudice has other forms. It may be that a more angry fiend is raging in my guts: an old, smouldering resentment for the superstitious saints that have tormented me with a sense of guilt— Mommy, Daddy, Maiden-aunt, sanctimonious clergy snarling sermons they didn't really believe, Sister Supernun who threatened to turn anyone into a pillar of salt if he dared look back, the backwash biographies of saints who went to heaven and sinners who went to hell. It may be that I want to reject faith just so all of them will be wrong.

But we can't let prejudice make our decision, either way. There must be some middle ground of free air and open-mindedness between the pressures of indoctrination and the prejudice of rebellion.

A new look, an open mind, an honest choice

The ultimate decision about faith cannot be the fate of a straw man, easy to set up or knock down, depending on the barometric reading of the present moment. We can't afford the dishonesty of setting up such a silly version of God and faith that even an amateur could do a clean assassination job. Nor do we want such a pollyannish version—normally fed to children—that no one in his right mind could digest it and remain healthy.

Our childhood concept of God and faith was, if nothing else, a child's thoughts in a child's world. God was either a Sugardaddy or a Slavemaster, depending on whom one listened to. We can't go on clutching to or clashing with an infantile version of God and faith.

We need, when the ache of the question is upon us, an open mind, one that is willing to rethink, revise, rejudge.

If we have learned this necessity of openness from our contact with other human beings, refusing to categorize them, or imprison them in a once and for all judgment, fixed and forever, then perhaps we owe the same courtesy to God. First impressions are often misleading, very often distorted, always incomplete.

Our ideas of God, faith, Church have been built upon a limited experience by a limited understanding. They may well have suffered from the pressures and prejudices which we could not resist. Our conclusions may have been premature.

This book is meant to be a guide to a new look.

I write as your brother in the flesh of our human experience. My own faith has been battered by doubt, frozen in long winters, reborn in a thousand springtimes. I would like, in these pages, to share my thoughts and feelings with you, to tell you about the way I have gone and what I have found.

The way you go must, of course, be your decision. What I have decided and what I have become as a result of my decision is uniquely mine and me. What you decide and what you will become as a result of your decision must be uniquely yours and you. I would be untrue to myself and to you if I tried to become just another pressure, trying to coerce an act of faith. A coerced act of faith is really no act of faith at all.

Stepping out into faith or non-faith can be frightening, if for no other reason than that you will find yourself somehow strangely alone at the moment of choice.

If I am like everybody else, if I have no feelings or thoughts which make me different, if I conform in custom, dress, ideas, to the pattern of the group, I am saved, saved from the frightening experience of aloneness.

—Erich Fromm, in *The Art of Loving*

CHAPTER ONE

The World Today: New Rhythms, No Rhyme

A Contemporary Parable: A group of the finest scientists of the day were recently commissioned to build a computer which could answer with scientific precision the question of God's existence. After completing the most intricate, sopisticated computer ever assembled, the scientists carefully fed the question into their machine: "Is there a God?"

After several minutes of humming and whirring, the answer came out. It read: "There is *now*."

Evolution: a complicated fact of life

It might seem strange, at first sight, that a book on faith should begin by taking the pulse of the world in which we live. However, man does not live in a vacuum. To a very large extent he is shaped by the world in which he lives and breathes and has his being. The situation of this world obviously conditions the possibility of religious faith. It affects the quality of our human interpersonal relationships as well as our relationship with God. To be ignorant of the inevitable contagion of everything human is to assume the proverbial posture of the ostrich, attempting to apply the solution of Napoleon to his critics and Calvin Coolidge to his unanswered mail: don't look and it will all go away.

The world in which you and I must resolve the question about faith in God has been summarized in many epithets. We have been told that we are living in the "age of technology," in the "age of secular man," and in the "post-Christian era." However appropriate these sobriquets may be, the fact is that, in our day and in our world, automation and technology have transformed the once placid face of the earth and have radically changed the pace of human life. The imagination of yesterday's comic strips and of the novels of Jules Verne has become reality in these our days.

The once naked eye of man is now empowered by the remarkable vision of television, x-rays, telescopic lenses, radar cameras, and electron microscopes. His ears have been scientifically sensitized by stethoscopes, cardiographs, seismographs, and magnetic tapes. His muscles have been amplified by all kinds of power equipment: power driven machinery, power steering, power brakes, mammoth cranes, laser beams, and guided missiles. His frail memory is enormously enlarged by the Polaroid camera, tape recorders, computers, and libraries of microfilm. He can even electronically produce human companionship, in the form of transistor radios, television, and telephones.

More and more man is coming into a fuller participation in the attributes of God. Technological advance has left him with a vague feeling that he is omnipresent, omniscient, and omnipotent. There is a new optimism and sense of exhilaration in him, almost an intoxication on the raw liquor of his new powers. Of course, his mansion on Mt. Olympus is only a part-time dwelling. There are tragic moments when his mastery over the world and matter falls short of his hopes. Floods, fire, and disease, not to mention war and other forms of homicide, occasionally take a cruel revenge on the pride of man. But the overall trend of his evolution is clear: man is taking charge, and will someday have the implements and the strategy to control the world. When he says, "Let there be light!" there will be the dams and generators to produce plenty of light. This is man's continually accelerating mastery of his world.

Almost always, and this would seem to be true of our times, the innovations of man bring him not only profits but also problems. Technology has forced man not only to accept change but also to accept challenge. Because of the rapid, if not planned obsolescence of almost all commercial products, there is an enormous spirit of competition. Laboratories and marketing offices are spraying the face of the earth with novelties of every kind. The pulse and rhythms of human life have quickened so suddenly that all who want to keep up, must run. To what we are running we cannot be sure, but we are making record time. New rhythms, no rhyme. New methods of education, for example, are now possible because of computers, closed-circuit TV and other electronic miracles. The real challenge is: What do we want to teach? The methods of education are waiting. The content of education is uncertain. How can we educate in skills that will be outmoded almost before the education is completed? How can those of a preceding generation educate those of the next generation for life if the way or style of life will be radically different? What in the past is of such permanent value that it must be transmitted? What part of the human heritage must not be lost if men are to remain sane and human?

While our philosophers meditate on these problems, the whir of life goes on. Spanking new expressways are drawing new lines of mobility across our country. Traffic engineers have put calculated curves in these expressways to save us from perils of hypnotic dozing at the wheel. We don't have to look for landmarks, since many of them will have been bulldozed between our journeys, but we have only to keep reading those green signs that flash in our upper peripheral vision. We have only to streak along in our space-age crafts, trying to stay in our own galaxy, right along with the modern asphalt ribbon. When the right sign flashes, we peel off. Automotive engineers have put a stampede of horses under our hoods, and these horses need only a gentle prodding of the right foot.

When we arrive home, we have only to press the button to summon the elevator in the high-rise. Modern technology has seen to it that the elevator will get us to our floor . . . 26 . . . 27 . . . 28 . . . without seeming to leave our hearts hanging somewhere in the shaft. The huge buildings in which we live and work have doors and fire exits, so that we won't feel like a Jonah in the belly of a whale. We just have to keep moving, as instructed, in the direction of lighted arrows. Engineers have figured it all out for us, have put us in the gun barrel of their corridors, and all we have to do is keep moving in the direction in which we are aimed, like human guided missiles. We can presumably trust all the electric signs and gadgets. We do not even have to stop another human being for directions.

Sometimes it seems that this highly mechanized, jet-propelled, staccato-tempoed Technopolis is moving man closer and closer to a national nervous breakdown. However, the Establishment has provided for that, too, in its vast building program that will locate a mental hospital within 90 minutes of every citizen. The modern Welfare State provides us many such friendly reassurances, but the problem in this society today is for man to be man. Living in a country which annually produces $974.1 billion in goods and services, we do not feel very affluent or important as individuals. The vastness and speed of the Secular City, and the orchestration of competition to which men must move, prey upon our psychological stability. We usually wait to get home at night to Pepto Bismol, to coat our irritated stomachs, or a little Scotch to unwind our scrambled minds.

Deep roots do not grow easily in the asphalt of our modern cities. Classic art has given way to psychedelic designs; Shakespeare is a museum piece, a predecessor to Capote, Metalious, Helen Gurley Brown, and Jacqueline Susann. *I am Curious* (any color) is alive and well and living in paperback. There are no heroes. We have lost them somewhere along our evolutionary way, whether they were literary, scientific, or religious. But so what? There cannot be any individual responses to human challenge any more. The answer to problems is possible only through the System or Establishment, which doles out money for research on various annoying human problems. People like Salk, Sabin, Teller, and Von Braun don't work for peanuts. Only the Establishment is big enough to back them.

Secularization

The prophets of youth have warned us not to trust anyone over thirty because they are not really altruistic or serious, just "finks" playing their games. This is the view of our society from the bridge of youth. It is a common fallacy among young people of every age to attack individuals rather than confront issues. The accusations of the young today cannot result in the verdict of "guilty by omission" without some sort of defense. Very much of what we experience today in our world is the inevitable result of the human evolutionary process. Social philosophers call it the "process of secularization," an evolution in which man has been engaged from the time he stepped out of his village tribe on his way to the Technopolis.

However it is defined, secularization involves a shifting of mankind's attention to this world, here and now. The Latin word *saeculum* means precisely this: this world here and now. The mentality of secular times, because of this concentration on the here and now, tends to deemphasize the *tradition* glorified in the opening song of *Fiddler on the Roof*. Secular man is not easily interested in speculative truths or ultimate destinies. He tends to be pragmatic and preoccupied with the task at hand. He is physically and mentally more mobile than his human forebears, and consequently does not grow deep roots in any set place or tradition. His hopes for a distantly future world and future life are only peripheral; his center of gravity is in the here and now.

Harvey Cox, Harvard theologian and author of one of the best selling theological books of our times, *The Secular City*, attempts to explain this phenomenon of our times. His thesis is that man's cultural evolution (urbanization) and his religious evolution (secularization) are necessarily parallel developments. When man's largest social unit was the tribe, and his resources to master the elements of nature very primitive, his needs and fears produced a "magical" type of religion. Having so little faith in himself and his meager knowledge of the universe, he had to repose his faith in one or many great gods who could know what he didn't and who could do what he couldn't. As man has proceeded in the inevitable advance from the tribe to the highly knowledgeable and skilled civilization of today, which Cox calls the Technopolis, man has simultaneously moved away from his magical religion, which sacralized the world, making gods of the sun, moon, and rain, to a religion of faith in man and his own powers.

The philosophers and sociologists who have most deeply investigated this phenomenon of our times see it as divided into three parts. The process begins with *the inevitable acceleration of man's acquisition of knowledge and skills*. This contemporary explosion of knowledge and skills has resulted in our current problem which Alvin Toffler calls "future shock." The future is upon us before we have the necessary time to become acclimated. To understand this first part of the secularization process, one must realize that knowledge and skill are something like money; the more you have, the easier it is to gain more. It is this cybernetic of acceleration which explains the ability of man to acquire more knowledge and skill in the next single year than he was able to acquire in the previous ten years. It is a certain projection that he will do so. One can observe a rapidly dramatic progress in almost any field of the natural sciences and artisan skills.

The immediate effect of this acceleration in the acquisition of knowledge and skill is the second step in the secularization process: *specialization*. As the amount of human knowledge and skill becomes increasingly more vast, there is an inverse proportion in the areas that can be controlled by any one man as a field of personal expertise. Consequently, individuals have to "specialize" in some very restricted area or part of the larger field of human knowledge and skill. A medical student of today can no longer ambition to master the whole field of medical knowledge and skill; he will have to specialize in one of the more refined areas of medical education. The same thing is true of the lawyer, the student of literature, and all the other professional people of our modern society.

Around these areas of specialization in any field of knowledge and skill there necessarily arises a "serving community," such as a community of surgeons, internists, orthopedists, etc. The law that governs this kind of specialization is as inevitable as the law of gravity. We may not like the law of gravity on our way to an accidental fall, but usually our complaints are tempered by thoughts of inevitability. The law here is that the larger the acquisition of knowledge and skill in any one field the greater is the need for specialization, and consequently the greater becomes the number of these serving communities. Furthermore, in such a society it is inevitable that the accumulation of knowledge and skill, resulting from an increasingly prolonged education, is that which gives an individual entrée into recognition, social status, and economic independence.

The third and final stage of the secularization process is called *socialization*. In this context, socialization refers to the interrelation of the various serving communities which were created by the need for specialization. These communities usually complement one another, depend upon one another, and cooperate with one another. It is this dependence and cooperation which establishes the principle of socialization. For example, chemistry will furnish the doctor with new and more effective drugs. Physics provides him with more powerful microscopes, better surgical instruments, and improved x-ray machines. Sub-atomic or nuclear physics will provide the doctor with radioactive isotopes, and psychology will offer medicine the fruits of its research on psychosomatic illnesses. Philosophy and theology will offer the physician moral clarifications, such as those involved in transplants, the prolongations of life, and decisions about the moment of death. Political science must furnish the doctor with national support and propaganda for medical research and government programs such as Medicare and Medicaid. Communication arts provide the doctor with a more effective means of promulgating his own knowledge, such as radio commercials about detecting the signs of cancer, as well as the means for more effective medical teaching, such as closed-circuit television.

In our modern societies, the cooperation of these serving communities is building tall skyscrapers and sprawling plants, and in the womb of these monsters is the perpetual tension of labor-management problems. We become acutely aware of the delicate balance between the serving communities today when we experience the crippling effects on society when the airline pilots or the garbage collectors or the telephone operators go on strike. In fact, any one of these serving communities can throw the whole alignment of society into instant chaos. Arbitration boards are forever bickering over this vital but delicate tension and balance that holds the Secular City together. Consequently, more and more human decisions are being made by the national government on the basis of computerized statistics.

The effects of secularization

Obviously this process of secularization, resulting initially from the acceleration in the acquisition of knowledge and skill, has conferred many benefits upon the human race. Some of them are right on the surface of life, such as new medical advances; others require a little more insight for detection. As man has learned to master more and more of nature's secrets, he has become simultaneously more and more aware of his own powers and dignity.

The secularization process has filled us with a fulfilling sense of accomplishment and has founded in us a valid optimism about the future. We have been transformed from lonely, sad, and superstitious creatures, cowering before the odds of chance and fate, and terrified by the possible dangers of disease, death, and destruction, into beings of hope. Man has likewise arrived, in the wake of this advance, at a new awareness of his responsibility for the world and for the destiny of mankind.

Because of the necessity of specialization, the process of secularization has also tended to confine men to their field of competence, and has urged upon them the distinction between secular knowledge, which comes from research and the power of human reason, and religious knowledge, which results only from faith. Those who preach the gospel no longer feel obliged to pronounce infallibly on all socio-economic problems. Secularization likewise has freed man from many of his old superstitions and delusions. Epilepsy is no longer misconstrued for diabolic possession, and insanity is rarely taken as witchcraft. It has brought the whole human race into a much closer communication, or at least it has offered man the means for such communication.

It is important to realize that the undesirable effects of secularization are only side effects. These do not result so much from the process of secularization itself as from man's unwillingness or incompetence to deal with them successfully. Among such effects, we could list *poverty,* since the distance between the knowledgeable and skilled and the non-knowledgeable and unskilled is increasing; only those with the necessary funds to undertake long periods of study can acquire the necessary education and expertise which lead to economic independence and a superior position in the secular society. The distance between the "haves" and "have-nots" will only widen unless we take positive means to prevent this.

Education is faced with a whole new set of problems, because in these days it necessarily demands an early commitment and a prolonged course of endurance to absorb so much knowledge and skill. The essential problem of education is deciding what to teach to prepare the young for a world that has not yet come about.

The problems of *race relations* are likewise aggravated by the process of secularization. Minority groups tend to suffer in this secular society because they generally lack the means or the time to acquire the knowledge and skills that are so essential to personal progress. But these and other dilemmas of this secular age must be left to competent sociologists. It is enough for here and now to point out that they are not inevitable evils, but must be classified as challenges encountered by

23

man in the process of his evolution. We will say more about the secular society as an atmosphere for religious faith in subsequent chapters.

Pluralism and the relativity of truth

If the phenomenon of secularization has largely shaped the world and human life as we know it, human society has also been deeply colored by the phenomenon of pluralism. Originally the word "pluralism" referred to a philosophical system which maintains that there are many kinds of ultimate reality. In this original connotation, pluralism was opposed to "monism" which holds that there is only one reality, either mind or matter, and to "dualism" which supports the theory that ultimate reality is of two kinds, mind and matter. However, contemporary pluralism is a kind of subjectivism, for which social dimensions of conduct are either reduced or eliminated. Each person is urged to do *his* thing. Reality for one man is not necessarily reality for another. What is right for one man may not be right for another. What is true or right for one time may not be true or right at another time.

Modern pluralism is based on the relativity of truth and is considered a sign of health among the citizens of the Secular City. This relativity of truth is not the obviously false doctrine that nothing is really true or false; it is all in the way you look at it. The relativity of truth, which fathers the spirit of pluralism and the acceptance of many points of view, is rather based on the assumption that no one possesses the whole thruth; no one possesses absolute truth. All of us know something about absolute truth, but no one knows it all. We know things about, we have glimpses of, absolute truth, but no one of us can ever exhaust it. What you or I see of the truth depends on where we are standing, upon our particular vantage point. Two people viewing the same statue from opposite sides will see two different aspects of the reality which is one and the same.

It has been said, and with reason, that the mark of the educated man is his acknowledgement of his ignorance rather than his profession of actual knowledge. The totality of reality or truth, especially in these days of the explosion of knowledge, is so vast that no one of us nor even all of us together can encompass it. Obviously the part which each of us can see will depend on our vantage point. If all of us are willing to pool our respective knowledge, each of us will have a fuller possession of the truth. However, if each of us assumes that his view is correct and total, we will only be engaged in an interminable and unprofitable argument. Through an open dialogue, society must attempt to cull that which is true from the various opinions and to synthesize all the individual glimpses of truth into a fuller and more complete body of knowledge.

In the Secular City, pluralism thrives in almost every area of human concern: in politics, there are various parties; in philosophy, various systems; in societies, various organizations; in ideologies, various hypotheses, such as democracy, communism, etc. All of this is more or less due to the secularization process, the main assumption of which is that no one does or can possess the total truth. In the Secular City each of what we have called "serving communities" comes to look at reality from its own viewpoint. And it is obvious that, as these communities proliferate, due to the need for specialization in various areas, an even wider pluralism is bound to result, and the relativity of truth is

25

bound to emerge more and more as an accepted fact.

On the level of the individual, the plausibility of one man's way of life may be challenged by the plausibility of another man's choice. One man's values will be challenged by those of another, as Peter Berger points out in *The Sacred Canopy*. It is difficult, if not impossible to avoid a confrontation of views and values in the Secular City, which has declared the principle of pluralism sacred and inalienable. Hugh Hefner can have and voice his own values and philosophy of life in the "Playboy Philosophy" with the same right and freedom that the Pope can articulate Christian values and philosophy in his Encyclicals.

Pluralism does not demand that anyone renounce his own life or values just because another does not see life as he does or cherish his values. Men will have to live with and work with each other on the basis of their agreements, limited though they may be. The atheistic humanist and the Christian humanist can cooperate with each other in alleviating human distress to the extent that they agree on the value of human life. Republican and Democratic members of Congress may agree on certain bills because of their alleged and common concern for the good of the country.

Pluralism and the relativity of truth which have come to be a way of life in the Secular City are obviously here to stay. The secular mentality views all human claims to the truth with a condescending tolerance and acceptance, but vigorously rejects the stance: "What I hold is true, and all contradictory positions are therefore false." The laboratory of human life yields its conclusions much too slowly for this kind of dogmatism.

The effects of secularization and pluralism on faith and religion are to be discussed later, but it might be well to note here that the spirit of pluralism is especially allergic to the postures assumed by most religious professions. Whether justified or not, religious creeds have historically implied that absolute truth has been confided to believers. God has entrusted his truth to us. Consequently, religion has found the soil of a pluralistic society an unfriendly garden site in which to sow the seed of God's word. This is especially true among the young, who have been born into the Secular City and who have come to accept the relativity of truth and the principle of pluralism as simple "facts of life."

As implied previously, the spirit of personalism is a child of the secularization process. The on-going acquisition of knowledge and skill in our secular society is possible only because men are willing to question all presuppositions. Nothing is accorded the status of certainty, and all knowledge is regarded as merely tentative. We have found out that the world is not flat only because someone, wanting to or not, challenged that presupposition. The field of biochemistry came into being only because someone was willing to challenge the pre-supposition that nonvital particles could not be present in vital beings. This kind of questioning has made posthumous heroes of Galileo, Darwin, and Edison. It has resulted in the birth of new sciences and given birth to a healthy spirit of scepticism and criticism.

The spirit of a pluralistic society can validate various, even opposed, viewpoints. Truth becomes a relative, not an absolute thing. All or much of this is very good. The problem arises when this kind of scepticism seeps out of scientific laboratories and invades all the areas of human life and existence. There can be no question about the fact that secular man worships at the shrine of the natural sciences, and when man begins to use science as a paradigm to question all systems and all truths, he may suddenly find himself in a very painful existential vacuum. He may suddenly find himself without a reason to live or a reason to die. He will begin to suspect all systems and question all values. All certainty will be corroded by his own ruthless doubting.

While this might seem to be a very healthy phenomenon, it is also true that man is not constructed to live long or peaceably with a methodical, universal doubt. Reasonable human existence has to be based on some certainties. The methodology of questioning all presuppositions and regarding all knowledge as tentative has proved advantageous for scientific progress, but the same methodology transferred to all the areas of human life could be fatal for man as man.

The generation gap and a collision of cultures

No portrait of the world in which we live and attempt to believe would be complete without a word about this sign of our times, namely, the growing gap between generations. Most serious students of our times feel that we are on the brink of a deep and serious change, heralded by what the young are saying and doing, by the rapid formation of a new system of values. Some of the more intelligent observers of the human scene contend that human society today, locked in the runaway iron horse of technology, is spiritually bankrupt, and will have to face an inevitable foreclosure, a deeper rift with the past, a radical change in human values and human behavior. It is a common opinion that we are now arriving at a point of crisis that could result in a total alienation and estrangement of the young from the old. And some hear in the strident voices of the young a pathetic plea: Don't let it happen.

Astonishing as it may seem, there are still some who refuse to admit that there is a generation gap and that we now stand at the brink of a cultural collision. The blindness and deafness of this complacency really supposes that everybody ought to be like us; there is a refusal to see that it really has become a different world and that this different world has produced deep changes in man himself. This is definitely not the world of the "Roaring Twenties," "the Depression Thirties," "the War-time and Post-war Forties," or the "Do Nothing Fifties." Almost without warning us the "Secular Sixties and Seventies" have sired a new and different generation.

Without a doubt, the secularization process, among a confluence of other influences, has produced a "new breed," more articulate, more outspoken, more critical and involved than any generation this world has yet experienced. Young people today not only have something very important to say to those who will listen, but they may even be saying more than they themselves know. The rebellion of the young is saying that man is in evolution; and this new generation refuses to turn back those mythical clocks or calendars to be "like" any previous generation. Man has, in this historical moment of his evolution, come into a new age and become a new man.

A recent newspaper editorial offered this reflection:

> Many college students leave school because they feel they are being prepared for just the same sort of life their parents lead, and they want none of that. . . . These young people are brooding about the failures of society, the void between what could be and what is.
>
> *Chicago Sun Times*

Author Konrad Lorenz writes:

> The industrialization that prevails in all sectors of human life produces a distance between the two generations which is not compensated for by the greatest familiarity. . . . There is, in our culture, an alarming break of traditional continuity between the generation born at about 1900 and the next. Scientific enlightenment tends to engender doubt about the value of traditional beliefs long before it furnishes the casual insight necessary to decide whether some accepted custom is an obsolete superstition or a still indispensable part of a system of social norms.

Everyone feels these pains, but it is youth that has arisen in our day with a special kind of prophecy. Youth may not be able to shoulder the full act of redemption, may not be able to tell us what we should do and where we should go, but at the same time it may be a very valuable function and service that youth is rendering. We are, as columnist Sydney J. Harris once observed, locked inside the steel ribs of our technological runaway horse. And it may be that youth is leading us to the only possible solution, as Mr. Harris suggests, by demanding an inventory of our values.

We turn now to a more specific look at the cultural collision to which we have alluded. Webster defines a culture as "a particular stage of advancement in civilization or the characteristic features of such a stage or state." Jesuit paleontologist Pierre Teilhard de Chardin was one of the first to sense the advent of a new culture, not a gradual transition or a simple introduction of isolated new elements into the old culture, but rather a radical break with the past and a new culture that will revere a whole new set of values and establish a completely different list of priorities. Sociologists, such as Philip Slater, in his book *The Pursuit of Loneliness,* insist that this new culture into which we are coming will not be a compromise with the past or a "golden mean" position. They insist that the process of evolution, which will inaugurate the new culture, must be accelerative to sustain itself. Liberal reforms of the existing system, with its motivational roots and values, simply will not work. They also warn that a prolonged, unplanned change could easily result in cultural suicide. The old simply cannot contain or resist the gathering forces of the new.

Slater, believing that the old and new cultures represent opposite polarities, suggests that the two cultures are built upon opposite assumptions. The assumption of the old culture, under which we have been living in recent times, is that the goods of life, at least those of monetary value, are scarce; and that therefore one must compete for his cut of the cake. Those who get the larger share are classified "successful," and, if they do so without violation of certain socially accepted norms which qualify and restrain the intensity of the struggle for goods, they are said to have "character" and "moral fibre." However, just as football players in the heat of the game are tempted to violate the rules, so men competing in the old culture for a larger share of the goods have too often reasoned that all is fair in love and war and the struggle for economic security. Hence, the easy lie, the soft steal, the understandable swindle, the acceptable bribe and the necessary compromise. Men were climbing on one another's shoulders for room at the top.

The assumption of the new culture is, by contrast, that resources are plentiful and that the supposed scarcity of the goods of life is spurious. Americans have been gouging, kicking, and clawing to avoid sharing a meal which is too big for one person anyway. There is no need for the kind of competition that usually results in aggression. Human energy should be spent on the cultivation of human joy and peace. The new culture accuses the old of hiding the cornucopia of satisfactions, and gathers its forces to release the bounty from its restraints. Consequently, there is a schism, a collision of the cultures.

In the logic of scarcity, men of the old culture girded themselves for battle, were willing to postpone gratifications, and found the expression of their feelings a luxury that could not often be afforded. They exercised restraint in clothes and colors, and in general exhibited a deep-seated fear of stimulation. The old culture was built on hunger, desire, keeping one's nose to the grindstone, and always reaching out for the carrot that dangles beyond. The new culture, on the contrary, depicts gratification as an essential part of life which is easily had. Resources are plentiful, and stimulation is not to be feared but experienced. And so the senses are bombarded by psychedelic colors and amplified sounds, by uninhibited books, and films, by bright clothing, spicy foods, intense words, and irreverent satire.

The "scarcity assumption" of the old culture has resulted in much structured inequality. The "haves" have somehow managed to figure out ways of legally prolonging their advantage, legitimizing their tactical maneuvers, e.g., by defining as crimes only the types of theft and violence in which lower classes, "the have-nots," customarily engage. The rebuttal of the new culture insists on equality. It accuses the old of making ends means and means ends. Instead of people working to attain goods so that they can be happy, people should be made happy so that they will work better in order to attain goods. The "scarcity assumption" has also led old culture Americans to seek out status symbols; envy of others and their possessions has become a basis for advertising: "You, too, can be a sport if . . . ."

The priorities of the cultures in collision could be summarized this way:

The Old Culture	The New Culture
property rights	personal rights
technological requirements	human needs
competition	cooperation
violence	sexuality
concentration of goods	distribution of goods
producer	consumer
means	ends
secrecy	openness
social reforms	personal expression
striving	enjoying (gratification)
Oedipal love	communal love

Author William Braden, in his book *Who Am I? The Search for Identity,* writes:

So it may be that the Humanistic Revolution in fact isn't leaping anywhere. With technology accelerating toward warp speed, people are just trying to get their balance back—to stand on two feet instead of one, so they won't be knocked right over on their heads, which are spinning

33

enough as it is. It may be that we are witnessing not so much a *revolution* as a natural and necessary *reaction* to a revolution. . . . The increasing emphasis on individual freedom and individual integrity must ultimately reject the notion of a single monistic identity — the idea that we are all really the same person. But the new humanism does suggest that we are nevertheless bound together in some sort of universal identity: that in some strange sense we do each of us bleed when the other is cut.

Conclusion

This has been a random sketch of the world in which nervous man, astride his powerful, nuclear-powered, mechanical horse, is ducking his head fearfully under low-hanging branches, and holding on for dear life. He is finding it very difficult to find the leisure and peace for the kind of reflection that is humanizing. Future shock and cultural collision are painful, but man is tough, resilient, and adaptable. He will, no doubt, survive, and the scars that he has acquired in the struggle for survival may someday be his badge of honor. In his present precarious position, the soft hymns and the quiet prayers of the past which once reassured him seem only like distant echoes from a vaguely remembered once-upon-a-time. He knows that his present momentum will not allow him to return to the past, and he wonders anxiously if the doubts which flood his soul at this moment in human existence will ever be replaced by certainties. He wonders if, somewhere along the way, he will find his God again. In the next chapter we will look more deeply into his mind and heart.

CHAPTER TWO

Man Today:
In Search of Identity

The effects of the secularization process and the cultural evolution described in the last chapter are in themselves good developments, but they have brought man to a point of crisis. To understand man in this moment of his life, we must be willing to look at his wounds. It would be more pleasant to pretend that everything is just sailing along, but the casualties in human society must be counted. Reaching for band-aids to cover the gashes is looking for patchwork remedies to specific problems. It is necessary to ask why man bleeds. We seem to be waging all-out wars against the symptoms, the fevers, and the aches of man. War against symptoms is futile; we must honestly face the cancer that lies at the heart of man. If he feels, in the face of the stunning accomplishments of modern science, some suggestions of his own divinity, he is also painfully aware that the forces he has created have cast deep shadows across his throne. Man, the Lord of the Universe, can and does feel very lost. The ambivalence of his emotions is uncomfortable, vacillating between the distant hope that human ingenuity will someday solve our problems and the despair of living with those problems. Human nature abhors a vacuum. And in this moment the ache of emptiness inside man is obvious in the shocking statistics on our national mental health. Two-thirds of all the hospital beds being occupied at this moment in the United States are occupied by mental patients. More than one out of every ten Americans has already undergone some form of psychotherapy. More than one out of every ten college students is estimated to be so emotionally crippled that it will be impossible for him to finish his education.

The Technopolis can ignore the moral imperatives of human nature only at the threat of its own destruction. Initiative and personal distinction, participation and commitment have given birth to the freedom we are supposed to know and enjoy. They must, in this hour, continue to define and defend our freedom. To relinquish values because of the complexities of man's civilization would be to sacrifice all that we have and all that has gone before. It would be a suicide course.

The distress of modern man has many labels. His sickness has many aspects. This chapter will consider the aching guts of man under three headings: *alienation, absence of identity,* and *depersonalization.*

Alienation

The most tragic paradox of our times is this: Man is discovering so much of his world that he is losing meaningful contact with it. He is gaining an increasing mastery over the forces of nature, and at the same time he is becoming more and more alienated or separated from it. He is simultaneously becoming a master and an exile. An honest acknowledgment of this problem is pressing, since man has only begun to unlock the secrets of the universe. We have already reviewed the cybernetic of acceleration by which man's scientific knowledge and skill will increase. Science is already predicting a future of controlled weather, controlled climate, controlled population, and even controlled human behavior.

At the same time, man is experiencing a progressive dispossession of or alienation from his world. The world that seems to be coming more and more into his hands seems to be slipping away from him. He is something like a domineering parent, who simultaneously learns to control and yet loses communication with his child. The modern astronaut somehow symbolizes the human predicament. He goes out to explore outer space, but he is scientifically and hygienically protected from any real contact with it.

Man's domination through technology has ironically enslaved him. It has projected him into his world and yet withdrawn him from it. The air conditioner spares us from the uncomfortable contact with the heat of the day; antiseptic hospitals quarantine out of existence, or at least out of sight, the miracle of so many human realities like birth, suffering, disease, and the inevitability of death. One of the most frequent and proud claims made for many products today is that they are "untouched by human hands." The human hand had once been so eloquent, expressive, versatile, and constructive. It was used to touch, caress, plant and reap, sew, feed, soothe, carry, defend. Today the human hand does not do many of these things anymore. It is merely used to push buttons, pull strings, throw switches, and steer wheels.

This is the dispossession of his world, the alienation of man from the reality of his environment. In controlling his world, man has put an almost completely effective technological barrier between himself and his world. His machines have separated him from life itself. It is not only the astronaut, the scientist, the engineer, the air conditioner or the hospital. It is the young person walking down a crowded street with a transistor radio blaring his private music through an earphone attachment into his private world. It is the family gathered together for a TV dinner before the set. It is the fan in the grandstands at an athletic contest, ignoring the crowd around him, a transistor radio broadcasting the game pressed against his ear. Modern man hears so electronically well and yet he is deaf: deaf to the needs and sufferings of others, deaf to the poet and the philosopher, deaf to the eloquence of wind and rain, deaf to trickling streams and roaring oceans, deaf to the silence of night, deaf to God whose glory fills the heavens and the earth.

If man knows himself only in relating to his environment and to other people, it is not surprising that this alienation from the world ultimately becomes self-alienation. This is the deepest human damage of our day, the cancer that lies at the heart of man: self-alienation. Pascal once described alienation as that which prevents a man from being comfortable with himself, comfortable alone in a room with himself. It is not surprising that people today consume sleeping pills in such enormous quantities. The agony of our insomnia is that we have to lie alone with our thoughts and with ourselves. The citizen of the Secular City hates a lonely street at 5:00 in the morning, if he is out there alone. The night lights are turned off, and the day people have not yet come out. The pre-packaged romance and the retail distraction of television are not yet available. There is no one to talk to, to do something with, to buy from or sell to. Only himself. There is nothing left to buffer him from his own thoughts and feelings; there is no barrier between him and himself. All the whirring apparatus of the Technopolis has been temporarily shut down. It has been said that this kind of aloneness is a good survival test and an interesting experiment. If you can make it alone with yourself at daybreak, the rest of the day will be a cinch.

Eric and Mary Josephson have edited an anthology of alienated writings, called simply *Man Alone*. In the introduction, the Josephsons suggest it was at the very moment of man's emergence as an individual, capable of forging his own destiny and beginning to unlock the secrets of the universe, that his present troubles began, and his person faced a new threat. It was at this time that he could begin to produce many big machines and build big cities. Simultaneously he began to lose contact with the steady pace of the world of nature, the slow rhythms of the seasons, planting and harvesting, storing for the long winter, and looking with tranquil satisfaction at the fertile fields that bore the imprint of his mind and muscles. The brutalizing force of the industrial revolution shattered all the old scales on which things were once weighed for value. Humanity began to die in man, little by little, inch by inch, on the assembly lines of mass production.

In the wake of this industrial revolution, man somehow slowly lost the ability to relate his skills and knowledge to the progress of mankind, to the skills, knowledge, and efforts of other men. His own work and person became devalued in his own eyes. He began to lose a sense of the meaning and importance of his own life. And once the sense of inner worth and outer meaning go out of a man, all real values and sense of dedication also go. The world becomes a thing of exterior ornaments, status symbols, and games. And all of these wither as fast as the flower in a lapel. Man not only loses a reason to live and a reason to die; he loses all appreciation and sense of himself.

In the age of technology, which began with the industrial revolution, very often a man or many men have been replaced by a machine. Besides the economic problems involved for the worker and his family, being replaced by a machine tends to corrode man's pride, his sense of worth and value. Nothing is more psychologically fatal to man than to lose his sense of personal worth. Little by little technology seems to have been moving man more and more into a world of psychologically lost souls.

In our own day, in the arena of the Secular City, we see man struggling in the storm of the inevitable. The bigness of the world which he has built is devouring man. The secular age is not only characterized by the ever-accelerating acquisition of knowledge and skill, but by the insistent demand of competition for the bigger and the better: bigger and better organizations, money training programs, marketing efforts, advertisement, research projects, laboratories, and humming computers. It is the survival of the biggest, because that which is small tends to perish, and so the law of the Secular City is: expand or perish. In the Technopolis it is no longer individuals but organizations that are contending for power and eminence. Moral choices, once personal and individual, are now available for the most part only within the context of the corporation or organizational structure. The individual is divested of power, and is unable to affect seriously the decision-making of his society in any significant way.

Through lack of such personal participation, man has become bored with his environment. Bertrand Russell once said that, if life is to be saved from a boredom that can be relieved only by disaster, some means must be found to restore individual incentive and initiative. Russell maintains that the ultimate value of life must be sought in the individuals of society not in the whole. If Russell is right, as he seems to be, what chance is there for the young of today to find meaning, to find hope? Men feel themselves trapped in the modern "economic miracle" of the Technopolis, the bourgeois Utopia that their ancestors so ardently worked to build. The modern welfare state leaves little room for personal idealism; it silences all dreams and the challenge of self-definition. It satisfies the nervous anxieties of the middle-aged through Social Security programs, but it simultaneously stifles the creative energies of the young. Consequently, many of the younger generation smirk at American democracy. They view it as a pretense, a big game played by the power structure for its own amusement, interests, and profits. The real anger of man is over his own impotence to do anything about it. It is this anger that breeds self-alienation, the most critical problem of our human society today.

As any good psychologist will attest, if a person is afflicted with a sense of his own impotence and insignificance, self-alienation and self-hatred cannot be far away. The self-estranged person is not only a stranger to himself but an alien to his world, and this is the soil in which self-hatred flourishes. Man learns to despise not only his uselessness and insignificance but his very self. And from self-hatred there is a second, almost automatic step to the hatred of others and especially of the institutions and Establishment that have made man feel so small. Man is something like a basin; when he fills up with anything, that with which he is filled is bound to run over the sides and spill out onto others.

The challenge of self-alienation broods like heavy rain clouds over the Secular City. The tragic figure in the center of the drama is man himself. A destructive malignancy is attacking his very guts, the muscles and fibers of his humanity.

The precise meaning of alienation is difficult and is more easily described than defined. Sociologist Melvin Seeman, who has been studying the phenomenon for the last ten years, suggests that the alienated are characterized by one or several of the following attitudes:

1. *Individual Powerlessness:* I have no control over my own life. It is not within my power to decide my own future. Destiny is in the hands of external forces such as luck or fate or the government.

2. *Meaninglessness:* My life is absurd, incomprehensible. Nothing I do seems to make any sense. Even if I would like to change society, I don't understand how or why things happen. Somebody must have an answer, somewhere.

3. *Normlessness (cynicism):* Normal methods don't produce results. If you want to get anywhere in this life, you're going to have to cut a few corners. Hard work never made anybody rich or famous. (This kind of doubt reflects the individual's low commitment to standards or accepted behavior regarding violence, ethics, loy-

alty, etc., and his general distrust of other people's motives and tactics.)

4. *Cultural Estrangement:* There must be something more to life than money. Whoever set up the priorities in our society ought to have his head examined or his books audited. I pity the kid who has to grow up in this country. (This is the classic alienation of the artist or revolutionary who rejects the goals and values of his community.)

5. *Self-estrangement:* I haven't lived up to my own life. I'm not all that I would like to be or ought to be. I'm not really involved in anything I do.

6. *Social Isolation:* I feel so lonely, excluded. I'd like to call some friends, but I'm not sure I have any. I don't really feel accepted by anyone as a person.

As Seeman himself says, "alienation is much more than this simple set of attitudes; it is an important historical phenomenon." The literature of our times is filled with many dramatic descriptions of alienation. The late Albert Camus, in his novel *The Stranger,* delicately paints a memorable picture of a human being caught and helpless in the grip of life, like a lethargic fly in the web of a predatory spider.

Our late president, John F. Kennedy, in outlining his hope for America and the world, once said that he looked forward ". . . to an America which will not be afraid of grace and beauty . . . to a world which will be safe not only for democracy and diversity, but also for *personal distinction.*" It is perhaps this personal distinction for which the Technopolis leaves little or no room in its margins.

Former Secretary of Health, Education and Welfare, and former president of the Carnegie Corporation, John Gardner, is quoted as saying:

> Our society not only fails to ask or to accept any depth of commitment from the individual; in a curious way it even discourages such commitment. Perhaps nothing is more effective in suppressing any spirit of endeavor on the part of the individual man than the overpowering size and complexity of the joint enterprise in which we are all supposed to be participants. And—particularly for young people—the sense of helplessness is intensified by the appearance of successful operation which surrounds the huge, glistening machinery of our society. It hums with an intimidating smoothness. How could any individual be needed much? . . . It is not surprising that young people shrug their shoulders and find something else to talk about.

The alienation of man, rising up angrily from his sense of personal uselessness and futility, grows out of the failure of our technocratic society to provide for him a sense of meaning and opportunity for personal distinction. Harvey Cox says that the symbol of the Technopolis is the *cloverleaf* and the chief characteristic of its inhabitants is *mobility*. The survival problem is for a human being to grow any kind of nourishing roots or develop any sense of personal accomplishment and worth as he travels at high speeds over the concrete geometries that shuttle human cargo across our country, winding in, around, and through our skyscraping cities. Human individuality lies as a sacrifice on the altars of institutional exigency.

The absence of identity

Erik H. Erikson, the world-famous behavioral scientist who never attended college, coined a phrase during World War II to describe the disoriented condition of shell-shocked soldiers who had "lost a sense of personal sameness and historical continuity." He said that these living victims of war were suffering from an "identity crisis." Later, through subsequent usage by Erikson and others, a sense or lack of identity was found to be revealed in the way a person answered these questions: Who am I? What is the worth of my person and my life? What is the value of my life for others? Achieving and integrating meaningful answers to these questions is, according to Erikson, the basic challenge of human life and the first step towards a full human life.

Most psychologists today believe that a sense of identity is related to one's place in his family. If the first child, for example, decides to be an intellectual the second may seek his individuality and identity in being an athlete; the third, seeing these other places already taken, may choose to become a humorist. If a child feels that he possesses no individuating talents, he may pursue what is called *negative* identity. He becomes the delinquent or "lost sheep" of the family flock. Negative identity reveals a "self image" that is negative. When a child or young person feels that he cannot live up to any positive expectations because he thinks so poorly of himself, he will gain his identity by causing some sort of trouble. He will not like to be told that he is really "a good kid" who has been mistreated or misunderstood. If his reputation as a "bad kid" is his only source of identity, he will part with it reluctantly.

The essential condition of identity is that there must be a sameness or continuity between what I think I am and the picture which others reflect to me (my "feedback"). My own self image must be validated by the reaction of others to me. Ironically, it is not only harmful to tell a person in search of his identity that he is all-bad but it is also destructive to tell him that he is all-good. We are so aware of our weaknesses that pedestals are uncomfortable. If anyone tells us that we are either all-bad or all-good, in either case the sameness or continuity of our inner perception of self and the picture we see reflected will be missing. Whether we have been cast in the role of "saint" or "troublemaker," we know that neither is a complete portrait of ourselves.

While the search for identity is really an ongoing, lifelong pursuit, it is most noticeably painful and vocal among adolescents, who usually experience ambivalent emotions in trying to grow up. Adolescents are not sure which of their mixed emotions are really their true feelings, and often adults aggravate this interior cleavage by demanding that the young make up their minds. What complicates the adolescent quest for identity even further is that young people are very often willing to settle for what they want others to think, a public image, even if it does not match their own inner self-awareness.

If a boy gets enough applause and recognition as an athlete or a girl gets enough whistles as a beauty, there is a danger that they will settle for this exterior image of the athlete or beauty; and both are in trouble as age takes its toll. The athlete and the beauty usually cultivate their exteriors so religiously that they do not cultivate their interiors. And obviously, their lives are over at 35. Probably the reason that most young people are tempted by this compromise is that the main fear of adolescents is rejection, ridicule, being overlooked. They are usually too quick to settle for *any* form of acceptance and attention.

To some extent the danger of adolescent compromise afflicts most of us in the Technopolis. We would be very anxious to be recognized and identified even for a single ability, appearance, or accomplishment. It is, of course, not the whole picture of the total person, but the achievement of any personal recognition in these days is so hard to come by. We are willing to settle for being the local bowling champion, the ladies' man, the best dressed woman on the block, or the man who once shook hands with the president of General Motors. It isn't much, but what else have you got these days?

In the absence of the essential condition for identity, namely the sameness or continuity between what I think I am and what others recognize me to be, I am cast into the role of an actor, and all the world becomes a stage, and life becomes a prolonged charade. Only one thing is certain about the life of such an actor: a sense of personal identity and worth will never be achieved.

What we are saying could perhaps be illustrated or dramatized in the identity of a professional actor. He goes his lonely way to the theater, where he sheds his name for that of Hamlet, exchanging his own clothes for those of a Danish price of the 16th Century. He surrenders his face to the ingenuity of a make-up artist, and his own vocabulary for that of a gifted man named Shakespeare. He paces center stage before a hushed audience of admirers, and in the regality of a name that is not his, clothes that are not his, a face that is not his, and lines that are not his, he ponders the dilemma of "to be or not to be." At the end, applause, recognition, and reward.

After the autographing and partying he goes his lonely way home. No one recognizes him. He sits with vacant eyes, remembering the pitches of emotion he pretended, recalling the recognition of applause. Those adoring people, his devotees, do not dream that he is as torn and shredded by duality as was Hamlet himself. He has achieved all his personal recognition and feedback for being what he really isn't. He can't wait to get on the stage for the next night's performance—to become Hamlet again, to be recognized again, to feel the warmth of the lights and hear the sound of applause again . . . for being what he really isn't.

Like the actor, many of the casualties of our technocratic society, who fool others by breathing, have lost their identities because they are willing and almost forced to settle for an act. All of us arrive at the arena of adolescence already bearing some scars of childhood: anxiety, guilt feelings, inferiority complexes. We have repressed and suppressed into our subconscious minds a great part of our own past feelings and history, and like all slivers pressed deep into and under the flesh, these things fester in our subconscious psyches. We throw up all sorts of defenses around our aching areas; we repaint our masks to keep our pains from surfacing. When the habits of our "games" have become ingrained, there comes a time when we don't even know ourselves at all and neither can anyone else. We are definitely sidetracked in our pursuit of identity and interpersonal relationships. We have forfeited the fullness of human life. This is the tragedy of non-identity.

Depersonalization: an existential vacuum

This age of technology, it might be argued, is not a completely depersonalized age. But the personal side of an otherwise depersonalized society lies chiefly in the "business-marketing-selling" structure. It brings men together in the common cause of economy, though it tends to transform the human heart into a cash register. Business unions, organizations, corporations are everywhere. The hunger in the heart of man for personal relationships is assuaged by clubs and societies, the meetings of which are the collected clichés and superficial conversation of "happy days are here again." They are comic relief from the cut-throat competition, crime reports, racial tensions, credibility gaps, poverty, narcotics, and the rising incidence of mental and emotional sickness. Accustomed to the belief that anything can be bought, the man of this frenetic age is rushing to psychiatric couches, sensitivity sessions, and T Groups, paying or begging others to listen to him, to help him relocate his lost soul, his lost identity, his lost person.

It is ironic that man should feel such a painful void inside of himself when he lives in a world of so many things which fill the air with sound, light and smog, but which apparently cannot fill the heart of man.

We have said, under the rubric of secularization, that the tendency of a technocratic society is to question all presuppositions and to produce a pluralistic world of opinions. We have also noted that man is not constructed to live long or peaceably with a methodical, universal doubt. Human security and the possession of personhood have to be based on some certainties. The methodology of the Secular City, which questions all presuppositions and regards as tentative all knowledge, has proved advantageous for scientific progress, but it has eaten away at all the roots of human certitude that nourish the life of man.

The absence of certainty and the presence of pluralism tend to produce among men an absence of values. Obviously, any value system has to be built on some accepted certainties. Radical scepticism undermines any and all such sets of values. A society in which there is no consensus of certitude is a land where angels fear to tread. It is an age of television talk shows and panel discussions in which the participants radically negate not only the opinions but the presuppositions of one another. Not too long age an actress (Susan Strasberg), a satirical comedian (Victor Borge), and a funny-type comedian (Pat Harrington) appeared on a television talk show. The actress was proclaiming the basic goodness of man, with a Stanislavski flair, contending that children are innocent. She proceeded to make an act of contrition in the name of the whole human race for what we have done to children by distorting their values, teaching them the ethics of selfishness, grasping, and dishonesty. The satirical comedian smirked at everything she said, resurrecting with a surprising seriousness the old line of W. C. Fields that "anyone who hates children can't be all bad." He adopted the attitude of the same Mr. Fields: "I like children if they are well cooked." The actress and the satirist proceeded to probe with surgical precision for each other's jugular, while the light comedian tried to turn off the high voltage with sporadic quips, once pretending to take up a collection from the audience.

Perhaps it was not really serious or memorable. But perhaps it did represent quite well the deepest tension of our times, the tension between conviction and scepticism, with most of us identifying with the light comedian, trying to laugh it off, pretending that there is no real dilemma lying at our feet. Having personal convictions in the secular society will certainly subject one to scoffers and to those who pretend that it really doesn't matter anyway. And a society in which everyone agrees to believe in nothing, as the lowest common denominator of peace, is teetering on the brink.

Without some belief in absolutes and some certainties regarding human life, there are obviously not going to be any values for which one would live, let alone die in peace. Once we admit the principle of scientific scepticism as universal, once we submit that there is no truth of any kind which cannot be questioned, once we agree that there is nothing which is really right or really wrong, there will be no room among us for convinced dedication. There will be no reason to live, no reason to die. Once the assumption of universal doubt arises it cannot be contained. As the Viennese psychiatrist, Viktor Frankl, maintains in his theory of logotherapy, man's most desperate need is to find some meaning in life, and meaning can be built only on certainties and convictions. The fragmentation and depersonalization of the individual does not lie far beyond the fragmentation and denial of his absolutes, certainties, and personal dedication. The questions ache deep in the empty hearts of men in these "the best of times and the worst of times."

The specialization involved in the process of secularization obviously leads man into increasingly smaller areas of personal competence and ease. The vast network of serving communities and the overwhelming stockpiles of human knowledge and skill are too much for any individual. It is extremely and increasingly difficult for any man to achieve a synthesis or overview of life, and consequently to achieve any integration of his own person. Anything like a cosmic overview seems certainly beyond the competence of any individual man. And this leaves him open to a dehumanizing, depersonalizing isolation that invades man like a fatal virus. Life is simply too complex, in the welter of all this new knowledge, for man to know what it is all about. If the essential daily bread of human life is "meaning," a sense of how an individual fits into society and this world, how he relates to other men, what he is doing that is of value, then most of us are suffering from prolonged hunger.

Of course a pluralistic society allows man a consideration of prefabricated overviews. There is Marxism, in either Chinese or Russian versions, Judaism, in Orthodox and Reformed types, Christianity, either Catholic, Orthodox, or Protestant. There is also Anarchism, Atheistic Humanism, Evolutionary Relativism, Zen Buddhism, to name a few. Or man can try one of the many forms of psychotherapy, since these have achieved something near the status of a religion in the Secular City. All these choices, however, usually confuse rather than enrich the average man who was confused to begin with. To accept any one of these overviews on the basis of an intelligent choice would imply a thorough study of each. This would be a monumental task, and one which is becoming more and more impossible while man has less and less time in which to do it.

Yet without some overview of life, some kind of personal synthesis, no one can find life truly meaningful or believe in his own personal meaning and significance. The man without some achieved overview of life will come into this world and go out of it without ever really knowing why. His life will become a string of beads; somehow all the things, actions, and people in his life will hang together on a single thread, but will not fuse into any kind of unity or coherence. Life will become a treadmill without any kind of consistent meaning.

It is this "existential vacuum," as Frankl calls it, in which human life is devoid of meaning, that fragments and depersonalizes man. In such a vacuum man begins to look for "kicks," ephemeral ripples on the stagnant waters of a stagnant existence. He may seek some avenue of escape from the vicious circle of meaningless words, meaningless work, meaningless motion. He may want simply to stop the world and get off, to cop out. It may be that he will journey hopelessly into the chemical paradises of narcotics or wander into an alcoholic fog; it may be just a matter of "beer binges," no real harm intended. It is just that everything else in life seems so artificial, contrived, and futile. Any efforts to commune meaningfully with his overpowering and vast world will seem like kicking discarded tin cans aimlessly down the alleys of an empty life.

Youth: Hope for an apocalypse

Youth is always the megaphone of the human condition, acting out what most of us feel, screaming out against that to which most of us have become resigned. The youth of today has been formed in the world that we have been discussing, the scene of life over which hangs the ominous shadow of the "Big Bomb." An educated guess says that there is only a 2% chance of the world coming to an abrupt, bright red end in an atomic holocaust, but for all their lives youth has been reminded of this percentage by testing on the radio of alert signals and a practice run once a week of the local sirens of emergency. Young people, consequently, do not feel much inclined to investgiate human or religious traditions, do not feel willing in any significant numbers to commit themselves to long-range vocations, even at these odds. Historical roots in a rapidly changing world are not important to the young. They are native to a world of novelties, change, upheaval. While older people are alarmed at the passing of institutions, cultural values, and tried and true formulas for life, the young have been conditioned to take change for granted. They have lived not only with the Big Bomb but with a perpetual cold war, in a world of complacent "haves" and rebellious "have-nots."

A great many of the young have reported their hurt by declining to enter a dehumanized society, and have huddled together in the search of human warmth. They have turned from the pillars of the past, like learning, dedication to ideals, hard-line religion and "all that jazz," in favor of astrology, palmistry, Zen, Voodoo cults and the magical-occult in general. They have seen all this talk about "law and order" as a trap. After all, the law has been passed down by the same hands that built this society. These are the hands that have fashioned the Secular City; hands that are stained by the corruption of bribes, pay-offs, political favors and dishonest deals. To them devotion to law and order seems a farcical solemnity.

Attempts to escape

Whatever might have been expected from an alienated, non-identified and depersonalized man, his search for some kind of relief has tended to turn him away from it all and to go in a dangerous direction: *inside of himself*. There is among the citizens of the secular society a clearly delineated and new inner-directedness. In fact, and especially among young people, this new inner-directedness seems to be the "in thing." On the outside there is a vast, complex world which certainly doesn't seem to need any individual and probably never could accept anyone who insisted on his individuality.

The world outside is a place of vicious competition, assembly lines, data processing, and mass operation. It is a question of either going out into that electronic wilderness or turning within. When man senses with certainty his uselessness out there, there is no other place to go. Out there he would be absorbed, devoured by massive systems and exploding knowledge. And the turning within only involves him in deeper alienation from both himself and others. On this stage many acts of anger or violence will be enacted.

Contemporary literature and philosophy are filled with the spirit of what is called "personalism." Personalism, like pluralism, is not easily defined. It is a philosophy of life that seems to have invaded the whole spectrum of modern thought and life. In itself, personalism has a serious validity, and is no doubt crucial in these times of depersonalization. It stresses the value of man over things, the openness of man to love for other men, man's powers, value, and dignity. There can be no logical argument with the stress of true personalism, though like everything else that is good it can be counterfeited in many ways. The spurious forms of personalism, into which many of the citizens of the Secular City seek to escape, are: *subjectivism, romanticism,* and *the cult of experience.*

Subjectivism distorts the true nature of personalism because it ignores the social dimension of man. No one can become a truly human being except in the context of his responsibilities to and relationships with other persons. Subjectivism of our modern variety is typified in the slogan, "Do *your* thing, Baby!" It implies a certain whimsical and self-centered behavior. When subjectivism is considered in relation to personal conscience, it tends to make each man a law unto himself, bypassing all acknowledgment of the demands of others and of

God. It reduces the complex perspectives of reality to the lonesome little world of the ego.

Obviously, the subjectivist will speak not of truth in itself but of *his* truth, not of good and evil but of *his* good and evil. For the subjectivist, being is becoming, truth is a matter of temperament, and there are no certainties available to man, only opinions and options. Truth tends to be a matter of where you are living, of your psychological make-up, and of your personal preferences.

Another contemporary counterfeit of true personalism is modern romanticism. As T. S. Eliot once remarked, sometimes man cannot stand too much reality, or, because he wants to avoid the one thing that is necessary, man is forever romanticizing his existence. Ionesco made the observation that man is forever trying to turn real life into literature. In search for relief from his condition of alienation, man today tends to romanticize things like friendship, sexuality, marriage, and the good life. He is turning away from the struggle-to-grow. Romanticism insists on instant love and idyllic marriages, and calls what is often a chilling exploitation and using of another's body by the romantic euphemism "making love." The escape into romanticism outlaws sacrifice, which is so often demanded by the needs and claims of others. The whole year is a perpetual Springtime; there is no room in a romanticized world for "the man for all seasons."

Finally, there is a distortion of true personalism which has been called "the cult of experience." The premise of this cult is that a person should experience all the things that are possible. The more experience one has, the fuller his life will be and the more developed his person will be. Obviously, no one can deny the value of experience or the reality of experiential knowledge. On the other hand, no one can deny the fact that all human experience must be somehow ordered within itself or it will prove fragmenting to man. In other words, a man must have a goal in life and must judge the value of experiences according to the goal or destiny he has set for himself.

To try to open himself to all possible experiences can only result in an interior chaos; it would break him apart. If a man decides to be a true husband and father, to be loyal and faithful to his marriage commitment, the experience of having a mistress or visiting prostitutes will make his heart and soul a divided city. If a person is determined to grow through contact with reality, which is the only way to grow, the experience of drunkenness or hallucinogenic narcotics will be very crippling to his personal growth. Becoming a person, therefore, involves the sacrifice of some experiences in order to experience more deeply the values which are connected with and which promote one's own destiny. Having decided what we want to be and want to do, we must exercise some selection in the experiences we seek, choosing those which are conducive to our goals and refusing those which could only detour us.

In our modern society these counterfeits of true personalism are broadly marketed. The subjectivists are irritated by any philosophy of life that will not condone "doing your thing," whatever it be. The romanticists are turned off by the thought that human destiny requires hard work and suffering. The pan-experientialists are violently allergic to any ethic that commits itself to moral commandments and believes in the reality of evil and sin.

Conclusion

Has all this been a little much for you? Do you feel that the world is filled with problems without any promise of solutions? Do you feel that man is supporting burdens that will crush him? Do not deny yourself the privilege of this discomfort, for then you will know something of how many men feel when they are possessed by fears about their smallness and inadequacy. You will experience something of the same sense of depersonalization and near-despair that they experience. Your empathy will involve you in the greatest challenge of our contemporary, secular society: to rescue man from his fragmentation and sense of isolation, to restore to him a sense of his own dignity and worth, to provide him with room for personal distinction and identity, to find the wellsprings of hope that give man a reason to live and a reason to die.

CHAPTER THREE

The Mood
of Man Today
and Religious Faith

In this chapter we would like to discuss the conflicts between the contemporary mood of man and the traditional stance of religious faith. We would like to examine these conflicts and look honestly at some of the aversions that smoulder in man and which incline him to slough off, if not openly reject, the values of faith and religion.

Faith and religion, of course, are not one and the same. The distinction between the two is similar to the distinction between what is sometimes referred to as the soul and the body of an experience. The soul is the invisible part, rooted in the mind, will, and feelings. The body of the experience is the outward expression of its soul. It is the putting into action of an idea, conviction, hope or desire. Faith, then, is like the soul of an experience. It is an inner acknowledgment of the relationship between God and man. Religion, on the other hand, is like the body. It is an outer expression of that inner acknowledgment.

Naturally, each of us perceives this relationship between God and man in at least a slightly different way. Consequently, we give different external expressions to our internal experience of faith. Those of us who believe that Jesus Christ is the Son and incarnation of God tend to express the soul experience of faith in the manner of one of the various Christian religions. Yet it is this very Christian heritage which modern man, afflicted with the myopia of the moment, so often finds repugnant.

Secular man views faith

Secularization has shifted the focus and concern of man today from an afterlife to this life, from the world-to-come to this-world-here-and-now. Secular thinking tends to turn away from the supernatural interventions of a God in a somewhere heaven to man's present responsibilities for his own world and destiny. Harvey Cox calls it a "pragmatic" mentality, which is less concerned with questions of ultimate truth than with the more practical question: "Will it work?" There can be little doubt about this shift of emphasis.

There is a growing concern for the secular especially among the young who were native to the Technopolis. Man is more concerned with the temporal than the eternal, more concerned with this life than with what the Nicene Creed calls "the life of the world to come." Issues such as peace, racial justice, poverty, ecology, education, and population control are more within modern man's point of reference than concern for an eternal salvation.

No doubt this secular thrust has received special impetus from man's new sense of power. He sees the horizons of his world continually receding before his powers to know and control. He has acquired a new sense of domination over the processes and problems of nature. To an ever greater extent he is learning to manipulate these processes and make them serve him. The limitations he once suffered from, and which drove him into cowering superstitions, have been greatly diminished by his own creative energies. The past no longer represents a wealth of wisdom and tradition, but it is a dark room he has left once and for all, never to return again.

Consequently, to be religious in the secular society means to be concerned and somewhat serious about human relations: race relations, war and peace, government spending, civic organizations, political movements, civil disobedience, boycotts and the techniques of the late Saul Alinski. Religious issues are: draft evasion, open occupancy, academic freedom, water and air pollution, and consumer affairs. Religious belief is belief in man himself, and the only real heresy, according to the secular gospel, is to limit man's personal freedom to do his thing.

Surprisingly, organized religions have been very obliging and docile. In the pulpits of institutional religion today sermon material has tended to center around these secular concerns. The preachers in these pulpits have been conspicuously silent about the indigence of man without God. Anglican theologian, Eric Mascall, in his notable book, *The Secularization of Christianity,* laments that "We have gone down without a fight!"

The secular case against religion

It is not just that secular man is too busy with the here and now to be concerned about ultimate questions of destiny. There is, no doubt, a real if subconscious resentment in him for the God who has allowed evils in the world and for his Christians who have seemingly done so little to eradicate these evils. As the philosopher Nietzsche, who first proclaimed the death of God, once asked: "If Christians wish us to believe in their Redeemer, why don't they look a little more redeemed?"

The fundamental argument of secular man with religious faith is this, that religion has historically been too otherworldly. Secular man sees religion as being more interested in another life, another world, another time. Religious people have not been conspicuous for their social concern. An examination of the Scriptures and Christian prayerbooks seems to confirm this suspicion. St. Paul writes: "Our true home is in heaven." Catholic missals once urged us to pray "that we might learn to despise the things of this world, and love the things of heaven." There is little doubt that Christianity has historically taken the posture of biding time. To secular man this can only be a fatal distraction. Secular man does not want a pie in the sky when he dies, but action and results in this here and now world.

The secular mentality tends to view the world of faith and religion as distorted by a superstitious supernaturalism. It is not only disdain for lighted candles and holy water, medals, and beads supposedly endowed with some magical powers. Apart from these admitted exaggerations and distortions, the secular mind has probed to the very heart of religious faith. Such faith, it would seem to the secularist, tends to regard human life as a concern of God and not of man. Sigmund Freud, in his book, *Future of an Illusion,* called faith wishful thinking and therefore an illusion. Even Dean Inge, the late "Gloomy Dean" of the Anglican Church, once said that "a religion succeeds, not because it is true, but because it suits the worshippers." There is no use trying to submerge the doubt; like wood that is held under water, it is bound to resurface. Submerged questions have a high rate of resurrection. The secular mentality of our day has reopened the old and painful suspicion that faith itself is simply an escape from reality. An old hymn once assured Christians:

> Be not dismayed whatever betide,
> God will take care of you.
> Beneath his wings of love abide,
> God will take care of you.

There are many occasions when a man does need some form of escape or consolation. Sorrowing parents, grieving for a dead child, or lonely spouses longing to be reunited to a deceased partner in marriage, would certainly like to "believe" that someday we will all be reunited in the house of a loving Father, and enjoy together the blessedness that "eye has not seen nor ear heard, and which has never entered into the mind of man to imagine."

Yet too often people who have called themselves religious have made their religion a separate department of life, an escape hatch from the difficulties of coping with reality. Churches have become places, in the secular view, where people can hide from life, where they can regard themselves as a kind of saved elite, or so it would seem, separated from and above mankind rather than a People of God in the service of mankind.

One of the more gentle poets of our day once wrote a verse called "Jesus Saves—Where the Hell Do You Get That Stuff?" A religious man himself,

63

the poet's anger was addressed to a minor league baseball player turned evangelist. The poet was convinced that wealthy industrialists had hired the Elmer Gantry type evangelist as a utility man to preach the opium of a bogus religion to the hordes of factory workers during the depression years. The poet heard the self-styled evangelist saying to his deprived audiences, "Don't worry that your stomachs are empty, or that your backs are bare, that your houses are not heated, that you bodies are racked with pain, or that your children are sick! Jesus saves! Jesus saves!" To which the poet replied, "Jesus saves — where the hell do you get that stuff?"

Sacred vs secular concerns

Some distinction should be made between the "sacred" and the "secular," between the sacred activities of man and his secular activities. Man is, in fact, preoccupied with the secular concerns of eating, drinking, sleeping, buying, selling, politicizing, recreating, studying, and socializing. For most men today, this is "where the action is." In contrast to these secular activities, there are the sacred or "religious" activities of man, which have to do directly with his relationship with God. The central of these activities are worship, liturgical celebrations, the sacraments, prayer, sacramentals, fasting, penance, giving alms, meditating, and making retreats. For most men of today these activities seem shadowy and unreal compared to secular activities. The action does not seem to be here.

In the areas of culture and learning, secular knowledge is that which has been gained by human endeavor, through the exercise of man's natural intellectual powers of observation, retention, and reasoning. The natural sciences, which quite obviously hold the position of preeminence in the Secular City, rely on down-to-earth empirical methods. They operate in laboratories, where men can verify their hypotheses with sophisticated equipment. More than this, these pursuits of secular knowledge justify themselves through practical utility; they provide better means of living, better health, more effective means of travel, and greater learning.

The methodology of faith is based on God's revelation, given through historically distant and comparatively indistinct events, especially through the life and teachings of a Jewish rabbi named Jesus Christ. There doesn't seem to be any clear account of logical procedures, nor is there any laboratory verification of conclusions. Consequently, these supernatural, non-pragmatic, non-verifiable, humanly contestable tenets of faith seem like vague, irrelevant possibilities to the secular mind.

In the orbit of the secular, man is viewed as autonomous, even if his autonomy is not absolute or fully established yet. While vague references to God are allowable, there is no real acknowledgment of any being higher than man himself; and so man must create his own values, set his own standards, run his own world, work out his own destiny. Nothing transcends his potential or intelligence, nothing lies beyond his own creative imagination and powers of actualization. He finds stimulation and exhilaration in the thought that everything is possible to him, and this inspires him to use his energies fully in the effort. He dreams the impossible dream, and rolls up his sleeves to build it into reality.

In contrast to this autonomous view of man, according to the secular gospel, there is the man described by faith. His is clearly a contingent or dependent status. His life is not totally self-directed but is rather a response to God, in whom he lives and breathes and has his very being. It is a response of acknowledgment that all that he is or has is from God; it is a response of love, obedience, and dependence. The believer knows that he is subject to a higher being and a higher will, which he will encounter someday in a "just judgment" of his life and person.

To the secular mind all of this seems to deprive man of his human freedom, his dignity, and his acceptance of responsibility. Consequently, these days of the secular age and mentality are not conducive to a faith commitment. Those who choose to believe will have to swim strongly against the powerful currents of human persuasion, because faith in these days may well seem to be a relic of the past. The pluralistic spirit of the present will allow some room for religious expression, but the consensus judgment of secular society will offer no sympathy to the vibrant faith of bygone days.

Alienation and religious faith

Since faith is basically a relationship of love, the self-alienation that is eating away at the heart of man is destructive of all true faith because the very condition of alienation implies that all or most relationships have broken down. No one who despises himself for his uselessness and futility can enter into a relationship of love, whether that relationship is strictly on the human or on the human-divine level. Self-alienation undermines all relationships, horizontal or vertical.

We have compared man to a basin, and said that whatever he is filled with necessarily runs over the brim of his basin onto everyone and everything around him. The person who is filled with self-contempt, a feeling of insignificance, can hardly engage himself in a relationship of love. He will project his own thoughts of himself into everyone else, and he will steer away from all self-revelation. The man who hates himself will most likely feel that God hates him, too, and that God is constantly accusing him of the sin of worthlessness. How could it be otherwise, if he is in his own eyes hate-able and open to this accusation? This concept of self is crippling, and a self-despising man can only cringe in the face of the commandment: "Love the Lord your God with your whole mind and heart and strength." Hardly.

Sometimes it seems that the basic assumption of preached religion—"Love, Brother, Love!"—is a downright refusal of God, his institutions, and his spokesmen to take us as we are. How can an alien-ated man love his neighbor or his God? To be down on love in theory would be like organizing a protest against Mother's Day. No one would risk that. But listen again to the voice in the pulpit, the voice in the gospel, the Sunday School voice:— isn't it really a living reprehension? Don't we feel more hopeless after a good sermon? After a bad one, we can at least ventilate our anger with good old fashioned criticism. It's the good ones that give us hell. They only make us despise ourselves even more. They make us feel that Nietzsche's famous reprehension to Christians is aimed right at us. The fact is we don't look redeemed, we don't feel re-deemed, and we wonder if we really are redeemed. All we know is our nothingness, our uselessness, our insignificance. And we don't need religion, Jesus, or Kahlil Gibran to remind us of it.

Besides this, churches are like everything else, big...big...big. They are institutions, and institutions are part of the Establishment. They compete with one another. They are, like everyone else, out to make a sale. It is so much easier and more healthful to play golf over smooth fairways and manicured greens on a Sunday morning. It is much easier to watch a sunrise than hear a sermon, especially if it is the kind of sermon that touches the exposed nerve of self-alienation.

A summary of the antinomies

In the course of human history, mankind has had its moments and moods. The world-view favored during one era is not always favored in the next. Insofar as the students of humanity can take count of the human pulse, the present mood of man seems to be in conflict with the traditional faith of Christians. The currently favored world-view is seriously different from the world-view of traditional faith. In this moment of human existence, faith and its theology seem to be in collision with anthropology. The obvious effects have been a noticeable lessening and challenging of religious faith. Those who believe feel their faith more threatened than ever before. They must struggle in resistance to the human contagion of unbelief. Those who do not believe feel like Saul of Tarsus, convinced that they are doing a good and noble service in ripping out the very roots of religious faith.

Here is a list of what seem to be the most significant antinomies or contradictions between the mood of man today and the traditional faith preached and practiced by Christians. You are invited to read them critically, and to make your own judgment about the reality and extent of the problem. History alone will pronounce the final verdict. For the individual only the moment of death will reveal the answer.

68

Traditional faith
vs
The mood and view of modern man

TRANSCENDENCE
vs
IMMANENCE

Traditional faith has been preoccupied with a transcendent God, one who is apart from and above the world we know. It has maintained that the knowledge acquired through a transcendent God's revelation is given to, not produced by man. Its chief concern has been for the whole world of the "sacred" and the hereafter, for the realities outside and above the here-and-now world. The truths of faith come from outside to man, from the transcendent God revealing himself and his will to man. Modern man, by contrast, is concerned rather with immanence, with the here-and-now world, with the secular aspects and activities of human life. Modern man is convinced that he produces his own truth; he is the author of his own knowledge, which is gradually achieved in the blossoming of his personal powers.

THE OBJECTIVITY OF TRUTH
vs
THE SPIRIT OF PERSONALISM

Traditional faith has stressed the objectivity of truth. Truth is truth and reality is reality, whether or not men recognize them. The law of contradiction is based in reality as it exists outside the created mind of man. For modern man, whose personalism has been so deeply affected by subjectivism, romanticism, and the cult of experience, the objective nature of truth is digested with great difficulty. While traditional faith has insisted that man's task is to recognize objective truths and to live by them and so to enrich himself, modern man submits that his fulfilment will be achieved through the evolution of his own gifts and his surrender to diverse human experiences. He does not want his truth on a platter. He seeks to formulate his own truth in doing his own thing. Truth for modern man is the work of human creative energies. To accept a pre-formulated faith blindly, to accept God's word simply because he has said it, is commonly regarded in our times as an insult and humiliation to the dignity and powers of man.

AUTHORITARIANISM
vs
SCIENTIFIC CRITICISM

There is really no intrinsic, compelling evidence open to the mind of man in his act of faith. God formulates his revelation and delivers it to his people; he testifies through his grace in the mind and heart of the individual man that it is really he who has spoken through the Patriarchs, Prophets, and Jesus Christ. The man of faith believes in the authority of God who can neither deceive nor be deceived. Modern man, however, has been born into an age of science. He lives under the ascendant star of scientific criticism. He worships at the shrine of the empirical sciences, and tends to become immediately disinterested in any supposed truth that is not subject to intellectual analysis and scientific verification. He is not inclined to consider a faith that shields itself from the probing of his mind by resorting to the explanation of "mystery." Whereas the believer must genuflect to the truth that God is not man and his ways are not our ways, modern man assumes that his own ways are the norm of human life. What can't be known and proved isn't relevant.

RELIGIOUS EXPERIENCE

vs

THE SILENCE, ABSENCE, DEATH OF GOD

Traditional faith has sought its corroboration in personal, religious experience. It has canonized men and women who claimed to have had forceful experiences of a loving God. The whole doctrine of "grace" is built on the assumption that God wants to and does enter the lives of those who are open to him. The biographies of historical religion are replete with instances of the presence and action of God in the lives of men. This is said to be an existential perception, like the taste of chocolate or the look of love. One has to experience them to know the reality. There is, of course, no psychological or scientific verification of these religious or mystical experiences of God. Modern man is simply not attuned to communications from outside his world. He is inclined to tune out all transcendent gods from outer space. He experiences, according to his own testimony, only silence and absence. His report is that God is dead. He makes the report with neither pathos nor any sense of tragedy. His interest and compulsion is to build a better world, and he seems to reject God and religion with a vindictive determination.

THE PRINCIPLE DOCTRINES OF FAITH

vs

HOSTILITY TOWARDS FAITH DOCTRINES

Faith in its doctrinal content has flourished pretty much on four products, and by demanding four

71

corresponding reactions in and from man: love, fear, guilt, and renunciation. We have already discussed the hostile reaction of an angry generation in response to the pastel-colored doctrine of "Love Thy Neighbor." Fear, guilt, and renunciation are also alien, if not dirty, words in the Secular City. Modern man is psychologically glutted with fears about his own existence. He is fed up with fear. He is riddled with the guilt of his own impotence, futility, and inability to cope with a rapidly changing world. He needs the message of fear and the guilt of sin like a proverbial hole in his head. He is having such a difficult time finding some sort of identity that the doctrine of self-renunciation can seem to him like a command to give up that which he isn't sure he has ever possessed.

THEOLOGICAL ORIENTATION
vs
ANTHROPOLOGICAL ORIENTATION

Traditional faith has been primarily concerned with, and begins its investigations with, God and God's actions. It is based on the initiative of God in revealing himself to man. In the relationship between God and man, according to traditional faith, God takes and God keeps the initiative. Modern man is rather anthropological in his orientation. He begins with man and his concerns. He is concerned with his own initiatives. It is a pedagogical principle that man, in the process of learning, must begin with what he knows, must start from where he is. Modern man is not oriented to or much interested in ultimate, eschatological questions, especially if they are about a Being and a destiny outside his own immediate world. He is too much sealed into his own human investments in the right here and the right now. He is too pragmatically inclined to invest much interest in the speculative questions of philosophy or theology.

A SUPREME FAITH
vs
A PLURALISTIC NOTION OF TRUTH

Traditional Christian faith has always been presented as supreme to all other forms of knowledge, an overriding reality, because it is the acceptance of God's word. When God, in his infinite wisdom, communicates his truth to man, man is not to question but only to accept. Traditional faith has presented the truth of God as monolithic, all in one piece. There is no other truth. Modern man, however, has a pluralistic notion of truth. Different people see the truth from different viewpoints. The pragmatic relationship of human means to ends is that in which man is almost exclusively interested; it emerges from dialogue and human trial and error. Modern man, therefore, is inclinded to resent the claims of religion to a supreme truth, a truth that is meant to be the norm for all human enquiry. He sees in this kind of religious complacency a rejection of modern insights.

A PERMANENT FAITH
vs
THE SPIRIT OF CREATIVE INNOVATION

Traditional faith has always presented its message with an attitude of finality. All revelation is definitively recorded in the Sacred Scriptures and expressed indelibly in the dogmas and pronouncements of the Church. This kind of finality in religious matters is not attributed to the powers of human minds or to the discoveries of human research; it is rather the product of the Holy Spirit, sent by Jesus. This Holy Spirit is the Spirit of Truth who alone can lead men to the fullness of truth. Modern man has an aversion for this kind, or any kind, of finality. His is rather a progressive, innovative spirit. He believes that all knowledge is relative and tentative. To him a faith that is permanent and indelible cannot be the hallmark of an open-minded person. Modern man sees such faith as fossilized and irrelevant.

A CERTAIN FAITH
vs
OPENNESS TO CRITICISM AND DOUBT

Even though traditional faith has carefully discriminated between infallible and non-infallible teachings, there is a nucleus of belief that is marked "dogma," and these truths, insofar as they are defined by the Pope or Ecumenical Councils, or recorded in some Church tradition, are fixed and beyond questioning. Modern man, however, reserves and insists upon the liberty to question every proposition and presupposition. All supposed truth must be tested by scientific hypotheses. Modern man has been conditioned to scepticism, healthy or otherwise, because the advance of his human knowledge and skill has been based on man's willingness to question. He feels that no body of knowledge should seek to exempt itself from these procedures. The very nature of faith, of course, implies the taking of the word of another. There is no possibility of a scientific analysis that could verify that God has indeed spoken to man.

FIXED FORMULAE
vs
FREE TRANSLATION OF MEANING

Traditional faith has not only categorized certain beliefs as dogmas, but has historically honored the very verbal formulae in which these truths have been proposed. Traditional faith is bound in expression to the so called "orthodox" formulae, the words of definition used by the churches. The Bible is the "Word of God" to believers, and Christianity has always been sensitive about any efforts to tamper with or edit the Scriptures. The "Word of God" is untouchable. From the view of faith, man cannot improve on God's authorship, and God is the author of the Scriptures by his "divine inspiration" of the human authors. Modern man, on the other hand, is always looking for new and better ways to say things, to translate in a fresh and more meaningful way the meaning of life and of man himself. Human idioms are constantly changing. The orthodox formulae of belief are largely framed in the language of essentialist philosophers like Thomas Aquinas. The idiom of modern man is most deeply influenced by existentialist and personalist philosophers. It is quite probable that modern man has not ever really heard God's word because it is repeated and repeated in a language that is basically "foreign" to him.

FUTURE ORIENTED
vs
NEED FOR IMMEDIATE RELEVANCE

Traditional faith and religion have been largely eschatological, that is, oriented to the future, to the future happiness of man. Perhaps modern man is short-sighted in many ways, but the fact of the matter is that he is pragmatically concerned with the here and now. There are too many insistent demands of the present to leave him much time or inclination to look forward to a future life, to an eternal life. Modern man is a member of the "now" generation.

INVOLVED WITH THE SUPERNATURAL
vs
INVOLVED WITH THE NATURAL

Traditional faith has always contended that no man can "reason" his way into or out of faith. Faith is a supernatural gift of God to man. No one can limit or predict the actions of God in his world or in the minds and hearts of man. Modern man, who is educated to be critical and challenging, can see faith only as a "blind leap," a life-commitment without any guarantee of rational inspection. He feels little inclination to proceed along such a dark and obscure road. The intervention of God in this world and in the lives of men seems to him to be truly a contrived and unlikely solution to the problems of human life.

EMPHASIS ON HUMAN DEPENDENCE
vs
EMPHASIS ON HUMAN AUTONOMY

Traditional faith has cast man in the role of the dependent creature, a humble servant of a higher power. Man achieves God's will through subservience and self-immolation. Modern man is mostly aware of his self-sufficiency, real or imagined. At least this is the way he wants to think. He sees human fulfillment residing in human exaltation. He sees the dependence of man, as proposed in the context of faith, as demoralizing and degrading.

SCIENTIFICALLY UNPROVABLE
vs
INSISTENCE ON SCIENTIFIC VERIFICATION

It is impossible to prove or to disprove the claims of traditional faith from intrinsic, rational evidence. No natural science can possibly prove or disprove the fact of a supernatural intervention of God. Those who try to prove faith take a self-defeating course; and those who would disprove it are equally predetermined to failure. It is consequently a futile procedure to pit faith against science. They are not and never could be in the same arena of contest. However, the stunning accomplishments and prestigious standards of science have led men to worship its methods. The methodology of science has seeped into all the other areas of life to such an extent that what cannot be known by scientific methods somehow seems to modern man uninteresting, unreal, and irrelevant. In previous ages, the man of ideas, the philosopher or theologian, was revered as a father figure and source of wisdom. Today he has been replaced by the scientist, the architect of the Technopolis.

CHURCH
vs
HOSTILITY FOR INSTITUTIONS

One of the main sins of the Church is that it is a large institution, and guilty by association of what bigness has done to man. Its doctrines have nagged at man, like a meticulous maiden aunt, rather than rescuing him from his despair and distress. Furthermore, the connotation of "Church" has always implied a group of elite saved souls, leagued in personal self-righteousness against the rest of sinful mankind. This is the spirit of triumphalism, recently condemned by Vatican II. Of course, there were always welcoming hands extended to the "sinner" if he would admit the error of his ways and come crawling back to righteousness. The Church, in its public image, has seemed a fortress or bulwark against the forces of evil and unbelief. Modern man finds this an irritating attitude. He believes rather in the unity of all men in search, in the search for happiness, peace, and brotherhood. He believes that all men should pool their resources to build a world fit for human inhabitation. The seemingly divisive stance of the Church in opposing sinners, unbelievers, heretics and other assorted categories of non-conformists says to modern man that the Church sees the world as its enemy, not as a partner in dialogue, not as a collaborator in the construction of a better world. This triumphal attitude of the Church, this winning team mentality, the "we are right and you are wrong" facade, may not be real at all or essential to the meaning of Church; but to modern man this is his image of the Church, and this is enough for him.

Conclusion: As to the future . . .

All institutions somehow identify with the culture in which they are embedded. The Church is no exception. The traditional faith and exercise of religion that we have known have been produced by the old culture, of which we spoke in the previous chapter. While the battle cry of the new is "Enjoy, enjoy!" the stance of traditional faith is marked rather by a "vale of tears" mentality. For reasons that are as difficult to locate as the conclusion is to justify, the spiritual life of Christians has for twenty centuries been deeply influenced by the notion that the created world must be rejected. However subtly it was presented, the denial of the goodness of the world was hard to hide, and the natural values of things were invariably subordinated to supernatural values, the secular to the sacred, this life and this world to the life of a world to come.

Strangely enough this prejudice concentrated most of its force on the human body, which was often portrayed in religious literature as the ugly prison of the beautiful soul. The primacy of charity in the revelation of Jesus was displaced by a primacy of puritanical chastity. Only with the advent of our recent "incarnational theology" are we in the process of redressing the imbalances of the past, reinstating the body, sexuality, marriage, and the joys of this world's good things to a status of honor. There is a gathering force in all the churches that would passionately disown any attitude of world-rejection. There is no room for the old dualities of above and below, spirit and matter, this world and the next. There is a lessening tolerance of the attitude that pleasure is merely a concession to the frailty of human nature. The strong revulsion among religious thinkers today for any such attitudes seems to be a healthy sign, and there is a new groundswell apologetic for the good things of this world that is supported most enthusiastically by modern psychology and theology. However, as would be true of any time of cultural collision, there are still painful pockets of resistance. There are still those holding out blindly for the things on which they grew up, hoping for a restoration of the good old days.

There are some non-believers who predict that faith and religion are today enduring a death agony, and that it is only a question of time. Believers are equally confident that God, who "holds the whole world in his hands," will not betray their confidence. From where I stand, it looks as though both camps are waiting to see the white flag of surrender raised in the other camp. It is a matter of prejudice arguing with prejudice, the irresistible force meeting the unmovable object. More serene and reflective types have opted for and tried to promote a meaningful dialogue to replace the "dialogue of the deaf" in which no one really listens and each side is complacent that it has the whole truth. If the evolution of man has brought him valuable insights—and only the fool would question this—traditional faith and religion must not be so myopic, so stranded in an ivory tower of self-complacency, as not to be open to these insights, even if they demand rethinking and rewording the contents of faith. It would be tragic if the central message of God's revelation, the relationship of love between God and man and between man and man, was lost because of meaningless haggling over organizational bylaws and picayune rules.

Christian faith could never be true to itself and its dedication to Jesus if it were to compromise the meaning of God's message. We believers must ask ourselves if we are really witnessing to and preaching the authentic message of God. Many intelligent believers, including the bishops of Vatican II, believe that the Church has much to learn from the world. The church has to be purified by the insights of the world if it is to be true to its vocation to be the servant of men. The Church must also be cleansed of all the human fingerprints that have obscured the legibility of its message. Though time may be running out, the churches seem at last to be aware of the necessity for flexibility and change without a compromise that would be treason.

One might speculate what would happen if the Church presented faith in terms of positive motivation. What would happen if human energies were enlisted in the causes of love, peace, and brotherhood, rather than being drained by guilt, fear, remorse and dread of punishment with which man seems to be saturated? What if traditional faith proposed a new image of God, immanent to and vitally concerned with this world, a God of love and encouragement living in and building with man a world of brotherhood? What if faith presented God looking with the eyes of great delight upon a "good world"? What if faith depicted man as the "lord of the universe," intended by God to use all his brilliant potential that makes him only a little less than the angels?

What if the hard and fast lines between the sacred and the secular, which tend to departmentalize reality and human life, were to disappear so that even secular reality was found to have a sacred dimension? What if faith openly acknowledged that its possession of the truth is in fact limited, and acknowledged its obligation to work with all mankind in an effort to understand God's truth more deeply? Old truths, of course, unquestionably remain true, but they can always be understood more deeply, and they must be applied to new circumstances and viewed in new contexts.

What if faith and religion portrayed a compassionate God, loving man as he is, in his human condition of weakness, instead of presenting God as the great Bishop of the Heavenly Chancery Office? Would modern man, in this case, leave his expensive and sophisticated gadgetry and rise out of his vacuum of meaninglessness long enough to go to the places of encounter with God, to be opened to the experience of God's power, presence and love? These are avenues of reflection through which our modern churches must agonize, asking with as much honesty as we can, if we really have presented to man only a caricature of God and his relationship to man and this world.

What if faith and religion helped man to find God in his own daily concerns, in the things that seem most real to him? What if faith revised its traditional presentation of man as a "sinner" corrupted by concupiscence, and rather stressed that man is truly made to the image and likeness of God? What if faith translated the reality of Christ into the language of today, and brought the powerful influence of Jesus and the touch of his healing hand into all the neuralgic areas of human suffering? What if traditional faith and religion were to relinquish all their delusions about a privileged status, and were to enlist their strength in collaboration with anyone who wanted to work for the solutions of human disunity and distress?

What if modern man opened his mind and acknowledged realities that are not scientifically testable and verifiable, like love, beauty, heroism, and the healing touch of God on the hurting heart of man? What if modern man were to reassess his own successes, and discover in himself a desperate need for the help of God?

Modern man is playing a futile game when he fantasizes about his self-sufficiency. Men are still killing one another in horrifying numbers. The bodies of the young are being torn up in the theaters of war; the Middle East, the Chinese-Russian border, Ireland and Viet Nam are powder kegs of destructive human hatred. It is more and more common to read about a crowd of onlookers taunting a sick, potential suicide into jumping to his death. We read about ritual drug deaths. Mental illness is rising with startling proportions. The second highest cause of infant mortality in our country is parental beating. The evidence is conclusive. What if man were to face this evidence and admit that he needs more than technological knowledge and skill for his sick society? What if man knelt again at the feet of God, reaching out to touch the hem of Christ's garment?

What if modern man were to invite the power of God into human life? What if modern man learned to pray? Yes, what if he actually learned to communicate with God? What if he listened to God with an attitude of faith and expectancy, believing that God really has something to say to him and a new power to offer him? What if modern man admitted he is not omniscient, omnipotent and omnipresent? What if he came down from his dream castle on Mt. Olympus, and admitted that he is a part of the glory of God which fills the heavens and the earth?

Only a lot of "what-ifs," you say, but these are questions that make for more than interesting speculation. What if there were a depth revision of the attitudes of traditional faith and modern man? What if they did enter into an open and meaningful dialogue? What if they gave up their "win-lose" attitudes to listen to and learn from each other? This is, we have said, an age of pluralism. I may or may not agree with you, but I would defend with my life your right to embrace and to profess the truth as you see it. What do you think?

CHAPTER FOUR

The Anatomy of Faith

We have been talking about the mood of modern man in conflict with the traditional presentation of faith. When anthropology collides with theology the result is always a lowering of the level of faith among men. While the attitudes of man, in the course of human evolution, are not above criticism, it is also true that faith can be and historically has been distorted in many ways by centuries of believers, preachers, and teachers. The body of religion has not always been true to the soul experience of faith. It is time now to cut through the too, too solid flesh of historical accretions and distortions to relocate the heart of faith.

Why do you believe?

Faith, like love, is an elusive reality. Most of the people I know "believe in God." They are also pretty great lovers; they "love a lot." I don't know whether it is my type of mind or whether I am haunted by the ghost of Socrates, but I want to know: What is love? What is faith? When the essence of love and faith is distilled, does it consist in having certain feelings? What happens to love and faith when there are no feelings? In everyone's life there are days when there are no warm feelings, and when God seems like a dim and distant reality, a word on the lips but no more. Can faith and love come and go?

Something in me wants to be a Socratic gadfly, wants to rip the guts out of words like "love" and "faith," to find out what is really inside. Many people are not like me. They can read the poetry and sing the songs of love without the slightest need or desire to attempt a definition. They can say, "Of course I believe in God!" without torturing themselves by any further probing. But I am a gadfly. I can't say "I love you" without knowing what it means to love. I can't tell God I believe in him unless I know what it means to believe. If faith really offers man a reason to live and a reason to die, I mean, if I am going to gamble my life and death on the option of faith, I had better know what it means, where it comes from and where it will lead me. I had better make sure it has a solid anatomy. I say, let's investigate. Can you live with me for a chapter?

I teach in a university, and when I teach I like to ask questions. I often ask my students why they believe in God, and I usually get answers that do not sound solid enough to me to make me want to invest my life or risk my death. Some of those whom I have asked about belief react to the question with the embarrassed announcement that "I was brought up in the faith." This answer somehow implies to me that faith is more a matter of indoctrination than personal conviction. Others react defensively: "I feel better when I believe." Shades of little Linus and his trailing security blanket. Others seem to think of God as a "good hunch." It doesn't hurt to hedge your bets. George Jessel claims that he speaks at Catholic, Jewish, and Protestant celebrations with equal distribution, because "one of them might be right." This is an odds-maker's mentality. If you go through the motions of believing, and roll a few cheap gifts to God now and then, it may turn out to be a very good investment, if there is a God. If there is no God, of course you are a loser, but the really big loser is the one who puts no money on God, and finds out that there is a God and an afterlife of reward or punishment. For me all these answers register a very definite: no sale.

The most common of the answers I cannot accept is the cerebral or intellectual approach. Some people give me the impression that they have thought the whole matter over, and have come to the logical conclusion of faith. I personally do not see how anyone who understands the nature of faith could presume that a person can reason his way into or out of faith. Aquinas and many other philosophers after him have held that you can prove the existence of an "Uncaused Cause" (God) of the universe through a process of reasoning that is based on the principle of casualty: for every effect there is a proportionate cause. But this is not faith! The Uncaused Cause which is known through the logic of the philosopher is not the loving, fathering, forgiving God who is known by faith alone. Christian theologians, from Augustine through Cardinal Newman and into our own day, have all stressed in one way or another that faith is not the result of a logical process. Newman insists, "Faith is not a conclusion from premises."

This same rationalistic notion is also used as an excuse for abandoning faith. There are those, for example, who profess that they have "come of age," and have, in their newly acquired adult status, sloughed off the "kid stuff" of faith and religion. These people seem to be saying that they have thought the whole matter over, and have tried

God and religion before the jury of their own minds, and convicted them out of existence. What these people usually are rejecting is a child's version of faith, simplistically confused with imagination and superstition. Any adult, who has developed some facility at intellectual in-fighting, can easily do a hatchet job on this "tricycle version" of faith. The essential sadness is that while these people have grown in other ways, they have not grown in their understanding of faith. It seems, however, to be a pretty common temptation to rationalize about faith, whether moving into it or moving away from it.

Well, what is faith?

Faith, whether it is faith in another human being or in God, means taking something on the word of another. It implies a new knowledge that can be had only by "taking someone else's word for it." If you explain a problem in mathematics to me, and I understand the explanation, I don't have to take your word that the answer is correct. I can verify it for myself. I don't have to invest any faith in you. However, if you tell me that you love me and that you will try to make me happy, there is no way you can prove this, and there is no way I can verify it for myself. I must believe in you and your word to me.

In the case of faith in God it is the same. God gives me his word or revelation. If I accept it, if I judge that he has really spoken to me, promising to love me and offering me a reason to live and a reason to die, if I accept him and his message of life, I have in that moment become a believer.

How does God give us his word? In the Jewish-Christian tradition, the word of God comes to us through a long series of historical events, beginning with God's word to a Semite named Abraham about 1850 B.C. and reaching its blazing conclusion in the word of God that is Jesus Christ. This word or revelation of God is summarized for us in the written testimony of the book we call the Bible.

By repeated intrusions into human history God has given us his word. However, this word is not subject to intellectual analysis or historical verification by the powers of human intelligence. No one can prove or disprove the reality of the word of God. Any such attempt would be futile, hopeless, and even silly. No natural science, such as philosophy, history, or archaeology can possibly verify that God really has spoken to us through the Patriarchs and Prophets of Israel or that God actually became a man in his Son, Jesus Christ.

The very most that human reason can construct are arguments for the credibility or plausibility of God's revelation. There are "signs" or indications that God really has spoken out of his own heart to the heart of man, but there are no proofs. When human reason has gone this far, when it has reviewed these signs or indications, it is called upon to make that surrender of faith which the philosopher Kierkegaard once called the "absolute paradox," and which theologian Tillich called the "utter leap," the act of faith.

Faith does bring us new knowledge about God, about ourselves, and about the world in which we live. But the peculiar characteristic of this new knowledge is that it can be had only by faith. It cannot be "checked out" by the powers of human reasoning. Once you and I are face to face with the word of God, as it comes to us in the Bible and Christian Tradition, we cannot prove or disprove;

we can only accept or reject it. Jesus becomes the two-edged sword that cuts right down the middle, dividing us into believers and non-believers.

But the hardest part of faith is this: in the absence of logical proofs, the only way anyone can accept the word of God is by a distinct and personal action of God on the mind and heart of the believer. Theologians have called this action the "grace" of God. God touches the believer in his own mysterious way, enabling him to accept the word of revelation. God gives the believer a new set of inner eyes to see what he could not see before, a new set of inner ears to hear what he could not hear before.

We cannot "psychologize" the grace of God. God's actions are outside and above our human sciences. We can know of God's grace only from its effects, much as we know electricity or nuclear fission. Somehow, in his own way, God provides his word for man, and then he touches the mind and heart of the believer, empowering man to accept his word. This is the most important thing, I think, that must be realized about faith: God takes and God keeps the initiative. God alone can make a man a believer. Our part is to accept or reject his initiative.

In the Christian tradition, faith is described as a surrender in which man entrusts his whole self and life freely, offering the submission of his mind and will to God who reveals, and who can neither deceive nor be deceived. Through faith man freely accepts the truths which God has revealed to him. He says his "yes" to God, and this "yes" is not mere lip-service. It implies a life commitment, a continual "yes" to the revealed will of God. There is, of course, no perfect human analogy for divine faith. But, if you have ever had to trust in the word of another human being when everything seemed to be at stake and your whole life would be changed and colored by your act of trust, you probably know something of the meaning of faith, the surrender, the utter leap.

I heard a story recently—it was fiction, I presume—of a man who had fallen off the edge of a high cliff. He managed to grab onto the root of a tree growing out of the side of the cliff, and was literally hanging on for dear life. He began to pray. Then he heard the voice of God asking him: "Do you really believe in me?" "I do!" protested the poor man whose life hung in the balance. "Do you trust me?" asked the voice of God. "Yes. Yes!" the man answered. Then the voice of God came back: "Then I will see to it that you are saved. Now, do what I tell you to do. Now . . . let go!" If you got the point of the story, you know something of the nature of faith, the surrender of all the human certainties and calculations to which we cling for dear life, as God whispers in our minds and hearts: "Now . . . let go!"

When Jesus rises out of the pages of the Gospel as a living voice, asking us to let go, his request is not something that can be fitted into some unused corner of our lives or confined to a Sunday morning ritual. He simply says: "Let go. . . . Let go of all your little plans for human security. . . . Don't worry about what you will eat or drink or what you will wear. . . . Seek first the Kingdom of God and God will take care of you. . . . Don't try to fit me into your plans, but try to find your place in my plans. . . . Make me your first concern, and I will take care of your concerns." If you feel a little chill of fear running through you as you read the Gospel, or you feel an impulse to look away from the challenge and talk about something else, it may well be a sign that you are beginning to understand the investment and surrender of faith. If it really hits you, you will have a sense of crisis, you will know it by the fear you feel in your heart.

The Gospel of Jesus indicts our selfishness and challenges everything that is good and decent in us; it asks us to relocate our center of gravity, to move from the prison of selfishness to a world of others, from egotism to brotherhood, from lust to love. It asks us to believe that the only real power in the world is the power of love. It requires us to love not only our friends but also our enemies. It demands a Copernican revolution, a metanoia or conversion. Once you say the "yes" of faith to Jesus and accept his blueprint for the fullness of life, the whole world can no longer revolve around you, your needs, your gratifications; you'll have to revolve around the world, seeking to bandage its wounds, loving dead men into life, finding the lost, wanting the unwanted, and leaving far behind all the selfish, parasitical concerns which drain our time and energies. It is frightening, isn't it? We are called to go out of ourselves, as though we were going out of an old home, a place where we once lived and felt secure, never to return. Once a person truly encounters Jesus in faith, he can never be the same again. This is the pilgrimage of faith. What makes it even more frightening is that there are no money-back guarantees, no road-maps that mark a certain destiny, no logical processes of verification. Only that voice, the voice of Christ somewhere inside us, asking: "Let go. . . . Let go. . . . Trust me. . . . Believe in me. . . . Let go." It would be too much if he did not also gently put his hand into ours, saying: "Fear not. I have overcome the world."

This is why I want to rip apart and examine the guts of faith. If it were only a question of intellectual speculation, I could live with superficial understanding. But if it asks me to invest all that I am, and in a real sense to let go of all that I have, to forsake my personal dreams of ambition for the Kingdom of God, I want to know as much as I can about the process of belief and about the God of faith. The rest of this chapter will be an in-depth look at the situation.

The beginning of faith:
The external word of God

> At many different times and in many different ways God spoke to our ancestors through the prophets, but in these last days he has spoken to us through his Son.
>
> (Hebrews 1:1-2)

We have said, and it is worth repeating, that in matters of faith God takes and God keeps the initiative. From his first conversion with Abraham to his incarnation in Jesus Christ, God has taken the initiative in speaking to man. This word of God to man holds a place of primacy in the process of faith. It is the first moment or stage of faith. If the nature of faith is to take something on the word of another, we must begin with the word that is spoken.

However, before looking at what God has said to us, something should be said about the manner of God's communication to man. All human knowledge begins with the activity of the senses. The senses are the antennae that take in exterior reality and present it to the mind and will. The remarkable thing about the late Helen Keller is that she could take in so much knowledge through the solitary sense of touch. What we are saying is that man's way of knowing is "bodily," that is, all his knowledge begins with the material senses. It is especially true that all human, interpersonal relationships are possible only because of our bodies and their senses. We are available to one another as persons only because of our bodies as media of communication. It is our only way to know. And so, if God is to speak to us, he must come to us in a bodily manner, in a way that our senses can perceive him. God deals with us as we are. Notice the sense-verbs used by St. John as he attempts to explain and share his own faith experience:

> We write to you about the Word of life, which has existed from the very beginning. We have heard it, and we have seen it with our eyes; yes, we have seen it, and our hands have touched it. When this life became visible, we saw it. So we are now speaking of it and telling you about the eternal life which was with the Father, and which was made known to us. What we have seen and heard we tell to you also, so that you will join with us in the fellowship that we have with the Father, and with his Son, Jesus Christ.
>
> (I John 1:1-3)

It was this way from the beginning. God came to his people of Israel in the thunder and lightning over Sinai, in the burning bush. He stayed with them and gave them a visible reassurance of his presence in a cloud by day and shimmering pillar of fire by night. He spoke to them in the audible, insistent voices of his Prophets. It was always in some bodily way that God broke into human history, and made the story of man the story of his own fathering, faithful love for man.

In the incarnation of his Son, God opened a totally new possibility of depth in his relationship with man. He became one of us. He was born the way we are born. He knew our hungers, and wept

93

as we weep. He ate and drank with us. He even subjected himself to the uncompromising law of death to which we are all subject. He was like us in all things except sin. In the humanity of Jesus, God was truly speaking our language.

What God has said to us in his word has been labored over and belabored by 2,000 years of scholarly effort. Different ages of men have preferred different emphases and have no doubt distorted God's word by the human inclination to interpret and edit, in the unsafe light of one's own prejudices. However, it is probably safe to say that God has told us about who he is, who we are, and the meaning of the world into which he has put us. Let us look briefly at the implications of each.

St. John, in his first epistle, says simply: "Whoever does not love does not know God, because God is love" (I John 4:8). In fact, however, God is not only love, but He is a community of love because community means sharing and the Three Persons in God share the divine nature in an ecstasy of love and joy. All love is always dynamic, restless, eager to give of itself. All true love spills over, is self-diffusive, wanting to share that which it possesses. And so this God, who is love, diffuses his life, his joy, and his love by creating us to share, by forming a human community of sharers. It is only the expansive, self-diffusive nature of love that can explain creation, your life and mine. It is only the nature of love that explains all God's dealings with man, with you and me.

To share himself and his infinite riches, God created man, formed him to his own image and likeness. The community of love in heaven—Father, Son, and Holy Spirit—has in creation willed a human community of love on earth. All human history and all God's actions in human history represent a gradual achievement of this intention. We use a lot of different words to express God's intentions for mankind. He saves us, redeems, sanctifies us. Sometimes the dust of theological speculation, distinctions, and refinements have clouded the central intention of God, as made known in his word. God wants to unify man into a community of love, wants to adopt mankind into his family of love, to father in man a new life that is a bond of union far more profound than blood-relationship could ever be. And all this God wanted and wants to be achieved through, with, and in Jesus Christ. "Yes," Jesus repeated to his frightened night-visitor Nicodemus, "God loved the world so much that he gave his only Son, so that everyone who believes in him may not be lost, but may have eternal life. God sent his Son into the world not to condemn the world, but so that through him the world might be saved" (John 3:16-17).

Try looking at the Secular City, with its alienated population, through the eyes of this vision. All men are brothers in the family of God. There are no strangers, no foreigners, no enemies. I am for you, on your side, and you are for me, on my side. We don't have to fear each other or be threatened by one another. We do not live under a law of the jungle, an eye for an eye, a tooth for a tooth. We have a new law: "Love one another as I have loved you." Sit with the vision for a long time and let it sink in. And, please, don't try the classic cop-out, you know, "It's nice, of course, but this is a cold, cruel world." God's word is saying to you and me that it doesn't have to be. I'm saying that, if we really took God seriously, we could have community in Christ, a family and a world of peace and love. I see the problems as well as you do. Even if we gathered a determined nucleus of dedicated

Christians together, what good would it do? I ask you to remember a Jewish rabbi of 2,000 years ago and twelve awkward fishermen who panicked every time a storm came up at sea. I'm saying that our strength can't accomplish the vision, bring about the Kingdom, but whoever said it was a question of our strength? "I will be with you all days" was meant for us, too. God and we are a majority. There is no one, no force stronger.

When St. Paul first caught the meaning of God's word, it hit him like thunder. He saw all the human barriers and barricades coming down under the weight of Christ's love:

> It is through faith that all of you are God's children in union with Christ Jesus. You were baptized into union with Christ, and so have taken upon yourselves the qualities of Christ himself. So there is no difference between Jews and Gentiles, between slaves and free men, between men and women; you are all one in union with Christ Jesus! (*Galatians* 3:26-28)

St. Paul calls the plan of God to unite all men, in harmony and peace under Christ, the "mystery" of God. This plan or mystery, according to Paul, was hidden in God from all eternity, revealed in the Word of Jesus, and is gradually being realized in the Church. Paul's development of this theme of human unity in Christ reaches its fulfillment in the epistle to the Ephesians. It is the main subject matter of that epistle.

> Before the world was made, God had already chosen us to be his in Christ. . . . Because of his love, God had already decided that through Jesus Christ he would bring us to himself as his sons—this was his pleasure and purpose. . . . God did what he had decided, and made known to us the secret plan he had already decreed, and which was to be completed by means of Christ. God's plan, which he will complete when the time is right, is to bring all creation together, everything in heaven and on earth, with Christ as head. (*Ephesians*, Ch. 1)

This is God's intention, and when we pray and work for the coming of the Kingdom of God, it is precisely this that we mean: human unity in Christ. St. John develops this same central idea of God's word in his "life" theme. Jesus says, "I have come that men may have life, life in all its fullness" (*John* 10:10). Through union with Jesus, God fathers a new life in man. John says of those who have welcomed and received Jesus, that "to these he gave the right to become the children of God, born not of blood or carnal desire or of man's will; no, they are born of God" (*John* 1:12-13).

> I tell you the truth; whoever hears my words, and believes in him who sent me, already has eternal life. He will not be judged, but has already passed from death to life. I tell you the truth: the time is coming—the time has already come—when the spiritually dead will hear the voice of the Son of God, and those who hear it will live. Even as the Father is himself the source of life, in the same way he has made his Son to be the source of life. (*John* 5:24-26)

This is what God has said to man in his word of revelation. The very life of God is to be shared in a human community of love, so that all men are to become as brothers in Christ. In being one, unified and vitalized in Christ, we are united with one another and with God. Through the gift of Jesus, the Community of Love in heaven creates and energizes a community of love on earth. Jesus prayed, in his last prayer before his death:

> I do not pray only for them (the Apostles), but also for those who believe in me because of their message. I pray that they may all be one, Father! May they be one in us, just as you are in me and I am in you. May they be one, so that the world will believe that you sent me. I gave them the same glory you gave us, so that they may be one, just as you and I are one; I in them and you in me, so that they may be completely one. . . . so that the world may know that you sent me and that you love them as you love me. (*John* 17:20-23)

This is the word of God, revealing to us our identity as the sons of God and our vocation to build a world of harmony, peace, and love. We are the family of God, and our work is to begin the real revolution, the revolution of love. God's word is a unifying, community-making word. No Christian who has realized this identity can ever be less than an individual, but at the same time he can never be only an individual. He is a member of God's human family and community of love. To the extent that he finds himself estranged from his brothers and sisters, and to the extent that he finds them estranged from one another, he is called upon to do something about it. This is the insistence of Jesus: "Love one another as I have loved you!" He has been given the fullness of life by the Father, and he has communicated this to us, and we are to share it with one another.

The basic understanding, that has been so blurred in the history of Christianity, is the vision of God as a God of love, trying to love men into life and trying to lead men to love one another. In the Old Testament the God of love assures us, through his prophet Isaiah: "If a mother were to forget the child of her own womb, I would never forget you. . . . See, I have carved your names in the palms of my hands so that I would never forget you." In the New Testament we have the incarnation of love in the person of Jesus, who asks us to love one another as he has loved us.

It is interesting and perhaps very significant to notice the trends in recent theological discussions. There is a new desire, evidenced in these discussions, to depersonalize God, to make him an impersonal being or force. I feel certain that this tendency is born of psychologically scarring experiences in the lives of so many of us. We want to make God an impersonal force because we fear that a personal God would be vengeful, threatening, petty and mean, more anxious to punish than to reward. The book of *Genesis* tells us that God made us to his image and likeness; but perhaps the most tenacious and destructive human heresy is our inversion of *Genesis:* We have made God to our human image and likeness, projecting into him all the aloofness, misunderstanding, harshness and severity that characterize our dealings with one another.

Phyllis McGinley concludes her verse, "The Day After Sunday," with these lines:

> Always on Monday, God's in the morning papers.
>   His name is a headline, His Works are rumored abroad
> Having been praised by men who are movers and shapers,
>   From prominent Sunday pulpits, newsworthy is God.
>
> . . . . Always on Monday morning the press reports
>   God as revealed to His vicars in various guises—
> Benevolent, stormy, patient, or out of sorts.
>   God knows which God is the God God recognizes.

The second observation to be made about God's word is that it is not only about himself and his love for us, but is about us and our love for one another. If God's word were only about himself and not about us and the life we must lead and the world in which we must live, it would seem irrelevant. God's word is a blueprint for life, life in all its fullness, and we must integrate God's word into every part of our lives.

Not long ago a clinical psychologist, Dr. John Hinton, researched and wrote about believers at the point of death. In his book, *Dying,* Dr. Hinton reports that many of those who described themselves as religious persons throughout their lives were horribly terrified at the thought of death. Many of these people were the type that had rolled their little gifts to God and derived from this a momentary feeling of inner security, people who blindly genuflected to all the truths that preachers and teachers told them were a part of their faith. They probably could have repeated by rote the orthodox formulas of faith they learned as children. The tragedy of their terror is that they did not integrate faith with their lives and the world in which they lived.

The word of God is not philosophical speculation about ultimate and otherworldly realities. It is not meant to be hugged and treasured like a hope chest of heaven. The word of God is for living, for loving, for sharing right here and now. A faith that cannot be lived each day of our lives will leave us destitute and cowering in the face of death. Faith cannot be a reason to die unless it is also a reason to live and to love.

God's word cannot be misconstrued to refer to another world, another life, another time. If this were the case, then the total relevance and the total reward of faith could be realized only after death. Man does not live only in the future, and he certainly cannot sustain a deep and genuine interest in a future-only faith, nor will he be able to make a deeper than word-level commitment to such a faith. It may be that this false presentation of faith as an esoteric, mysterious treasure, carefully insulated from contact with daily life, accounts for some of the contemporary disinterest in religion and faith. As John Courtney Murray, in his book, *The Problem of God,* points out, many people today have simply lost interest in arguing about God and an afterlife. If people today have simply lost interest, it is probably because their professed interest is in doing something about the problems, the distress and the evil that afflict man in the here and now. The supposed fact that God's in his heaven definitely does not make all well with the world, which aches and hurts to the marrow of its bones.

And this is precisely the challenge of the word of God, which looks not only *beyond* this world but deeply *into* this world. The word of God is perhaps the most definitive statement ever made about the meaning of this world and the meaning of human existence in this world. It provides a vision and perspective which rescues us from our delusions and unknots the shackles of our prejudices. It helps us understand what is really important and what is really unimportant.

How does this vision and perspective result from hearing the word of God? By some kind of programing all of us are necessarily selective in our perception of reality. For example, if a scientist and an artist walk down the same street together, the chances are they will notice very different things. Their temperaments and training have made them more aware of different aspects of reality. Almost everything depends, in our perception of reality, on what we think is important. These things become our life values. In his word of revelation, God is telling us what is really important and what is unimportant. We are the beneficiaries of his infinite wisdom which helps us to see ourselves and our world in accurate focus.

It is difficult for most of us to admit, but we are creatures of delusion. We tend to confuse the important things in life with the unimportant, to expend our emotional energies on trivialities while we remain apathetic about the serious tragedies that afflict our human family. God's word is a summons to reality. Most of all it calls us out of an egocentric existence, out of the small and self-centered world that has a population of one. Whatever else God's word to man might mean, this much is true: unless it invades, shapes, turns inside out our values and daily lives, it will be a sterile word. It will be a seed that has fallen on exhausted ground.

Obviously, God's word is not for those who seek only that tranquil peace of compromise which results from everybody agreeing to believe in nothing. This would be a tragic common denominator. God's word is for the creative, the strong, for those who dream impossible dreams and reach for unreachable stars, such as a new world for man, a human family and a community of love. The personalized word of God, Jesus, is the man for others, who calls us from the tyranny of egotism into the freedom of brotherhood, here in this world and at this time.

The internal word of God

> Then Simon Peter spoke up: "You are the Messiah, the Son of the living God." "Good for you, Simon, son of John!" answered Jesus. "Because this truth did not come to you from any human being or your own human resources. It was given to you directly by my Father in heaven." (*Matthew* 16:16-17)

We have been talking about the word of God that has been spoken to us through the Patriarchs, Prophets, and the Son of God. We have said that this word lies beyond all possibility of scientific proof. Human reason alone is helpless to accept or reject it. Only through a new action of God on the mind and heart of the believer can anyone be led into faith. When Peter, in the familiar passage from the New Testament quoted above, proclaims the Messiahship and divinity of Jesus, Jesus is quick to congratulate him because the human mind with all of its natural powers and resources has no power to know these truths. This kind of knowledge, Jesus is saying, can be had only through an interior revelation of God. This is the interior word of God, which is an essential part of the grace of faith. God himself must somehow testify inside the human heart and mind: "This word of the Bible is my word. I give you my own assurance."

The Bible certainly cannot be classified as objective history, and there are no other contemporary historical documents to confirm the historicity of all the events related to us in the Bible. The word of God in the Bible, which we have called the external word of God, tells us that a transcendent God has become immanent in our world, and has called us to human unity in Christ his Son; it has summoned us to roll up our sleeves and get down to the work of achieving this plan of God, to bring about his Kingdom, which marches at the pace of men's feet. God has made human history the history of his own love, and we must be the catalysts or channels of that love to all men. The human mind and our natural sciences cannot recognize the reality of this vision given to us by the word of God. Only the eyes of faith see this vision, and God alone can make a man a believer.

How does God testify within us? How does God bring a non-believer into belief? While his ways are always marked by mystery, there are three things which we must understand if we are to understand the meaning of the interior word of God: (1) the hunger in the heart of all men for God, (2) the attraction of God in the human will, and (3) the illumination by God of the human mind.

All of us are willing to admit pangs of hunger and feelings of emptiness inside us. We experience half-formed dreams and vague drives for something more than human resources can promise or produce. There is in each of us a dynamic, a mystique or drive that, unless detoured by human selfishness, leads us to search for God, whether we know it or not. It is this desire that carries us beyond what we can see into the darkness and obscurity of faith. It is a hunger that can be satisfied in God alone. Obviously, God does not intend to satisfy this desire completely in this world; its function is to draw us closer and closer to God who alone can give us complete satisfaction. This is the truth which St. Augustine discovered, after the discouragement of so many blind alleys: "Our hearts were made for you, O God, and they shall not rest until they rest in you."

Dr. Karl Stern, the Jewish psychiatrist who told the story of his conversion to Christ in his book, *Pillar of Fire,* writes:

> Now we encounter that principle of eternal longing, of the "never-quite-fulfilled" again in the transcendence of the human personality. St. Gregory of Nyssa comments: ". . . for the desire of those who thus rise never rests in what they can already understand; but by an ever greater desire, the soul keeps rising constantly to another which lies ahead, and thus it makes its way through the ever higher regions towards the transcendent God." In other words, man has been created a God-addict.

Dr. Stern goes on to say that one thing has become quite clear to him from his experience as a psychiatrist, that there is something "unstillable" in man, a sense of hunger that is always pushing man in the direction of God. He quotes the poet Goethe's version of Augustine's discovery: "All urge and struggle means eternal longing for God, the Lord." The beginning of God's internal word is a void or hunger, like the question which precedes an answer, like the darkness that awaits the coming of light.

There is no single way that this hunger for God will manifest itself concretely. The important realization is that, even in these desires of man, God has already begun the work of faith. He leads men from this instinct which he has implanted in human nature in whatever way he chooses. The specific hungers which individual men experience will differ according to their character, temperament, inclinations, social influences, and environment. But always, the interior word of God begins with a hunger, an emptiness, a need. Karl Rahner, in his book *Prayer,* says that, when we experience this painful emptiness, we can feel sure that we are already being drawn by God. All of us are born into the condition of reaching beyond ourselves.

Another psyciatrist, Dr. Frederick von Gagern, in his book, *Mental and Spiritual Health,* writes:

> Man is so made that he strives always toward a "good" that seems to him worthy of his effort. This may be near or remote, tangible or ideal, animal or spiritual. He may be in error; but he strives, in his own way towards a fulfillment. In a rightly ordered life, the struggle is towards perfection, the only final real good: God.

> To translate our yearning into action, we need not only the will to do so, but also the psychic energy. All terms such as instinct, instinctive force, motive force or vitality are, basically, just so many different words for the same dynamic energy of the soul, the energy that drives us forward towards a goal. This vitality or force of instinct, call it what you will, is the motor driving us beyond ourselves, and, if we keep on the road, to God.

> It must never be forgotten that it is precisely here, in the depths of the non-rational self, that God has planted the seeds of our growth towards perfection and fulfillment. All of us may profitably realize that theology, operating from above downwards, arrives at the same conclusions as anthropology, building from the bottom upwards.

Having been born with these drives implanted in us, this is precisely where God's action on the will or desires enters into the total process of believing. While faith is essentially an act of the mind, a judgment that God's external word or revelation is true, it is the will which God first touches by his grace in some form of attraction to the good, even if this good is not consciously recognized as an attraction to God himself.

The experience of God touching and involving the human will in search may come to different men in different ways. There are many avenues of attraction to God. Some are drawn to him through his beauty, others to his peace, and still others are attracted by his power. Most men find themselves drawn to God as the source and wellspring of the very meaning of life, the ultimate ground of human existence. But it may be that the first motion of God within the believer-to-be is one of disturbance. Sometimes we forget that God comes to us, not only to give us peace but also to disturb us. He comforts the afflicted and he afflicts the comfortable. For some men life becomes a hopeless mess, and they find themselves aware of a demand to know what it is all about. This inner restlessness and disquiet can well be God sowing the first seeds of faith in the human heart.

God, however, is not coercive. It may be that the seeds of desire sown in the human heart will never grow deeper roots or find satisfaction. Jesus said that some seed falls upon fertile ground and some falls upon shallow ground where it dies. Sometimes the action of God within the human will seems to be snuffed out in an act of despair or bitterness. All of us have at some time been unresponsive to God and his grace. But almost always the attraction will turn up again in some new way and in some new place. There will be a new moral conflict, a new personal problem, a new human relationship, a new responsibility to be borne, or a new decision to be made. There is such a deep hunger in man for God that, even if the renewed attraction of God is pushed aside, it will return again, perhaps even stronger, more deeply moving, or more inwardly disturbing.

Once these desires begin to grow in the man of good will, through the anonymous and undefinable attraction of God, it is usual that grace then begins to influence the intellect. The first signs of grace in the intellect are usually the eruption of doubt and debate. Things may seem very clear in one moment and then all clarity can seem to disappear in the next. There are alternating periods of involvement with the question of faith and perhaps utter indifference.

It is not uncommon for a person in this stage to feel like a dual personality, highly enthusiastic about the pursuit of God one day and strangely cold and unmoved by the thought of God the next day. Through the maze of all these turns, sometimes after a considerable lapse of time, one day the mind will be filled with the realization that God really exists, that he really cares, and that his love is asking for a response in our lives. Faith may either be discovered for the first time in this way or rediscovered after it has been put aside. It is on the basis of his experience, whatever form that experience may take, that one day a man finds himself ready to commit himself: I believe.

The act of faith

St. Thomas Aquinas says in *De Veritate:* "It is God who causes faith in the believer by prompting his will and enlightening his intellect." In the act of faith the believer accepts the external word of God because God has spoken an internal word of confirmation in his heart and mind. Graced by God in his will and intellect, the believer makes an intellectual judgment that is the act of faith. He says "yes" to God. He says: "I believe!" He is convinced that the external word of God, calling us to human unity in Christ, is truly the word of God spoken to man.

It should be noticed that the act of faith is a judgment made by the mind. And since there are degrees of certainty in the judgments of our minds, it may be that at first faith may seem a tremulous and quivering judgment. One can never program the grace of God, but the usual experience of initial faith-commitment is not one that immediately penetrates the marrow of the bones. However, to the extent that the believer really means it, he can never be the same again.

Very often people want to locate faith in the realm of sentiment or feelings, to strip it of all intellectual content. Following Martin Luther, some have tried to distinguish between "faith" and "belief." In this distinction, faith is an act of God in us that makes us adhere to him, and belief is simply the human formulation of this experience, something inadequate, fluctuating and changing. Such a distinction tends to move faith out of the sphere of definite knowledge and into the sphere of an emotional religious experience for which one can never quite find the right descriptive words. No one reasons his way into or out of faith, but faith, mysterious as its origins may be, is a matter of definite knowledge about God, ourselves, and about our world. If these truths of God's external word were in no way intelligible to us, faith would offer no support to our lives. Eugene Joly, in his book *What is Faith?*, remarks:

> A mystery is not a wall against which you run your head, but an ocean into which you plunge. A mystery is not night; it is the sun, so brilliant that we cannot gaze at it, but so luminous that everything is illuminated by it.

In the act of faith, the motive or moving force is God himself who has spoken both his external word to all men and his internal word inside the will and mind of the believer. In almost all of the other judgments of truth that we make, the motive is our perception of available evidence. We gather in evidence, evaluate it, and finally come to our conclusion. The process of faith is quite different. There simply is no conclusive evidence available to our minds. We cannot reason our way into faith as we reason our way to other conclusions. It is simply a conclusion that results from God's attraction in the will and his enlightenment of the intellect.

In making an act of faith man has to trust his own experience of God, whom he has experienced in his mind and heart. However, while he must ultimately make some kind of "blind leap," he does not act against reason. The blindness of faith does not imply irrationality. In crossing the chasm into the world of faith, man does surpass the limits of his own reasoning powers, but only through an utter reliance on the God who has already acted within him. His reason does not possess a road map to the destiny of faith, but he is confident that another hand is really in his, and that he is not throwing himself into a black void but rather into the arms of Someone who loves him. God has spoken a living, loving word within him and he has responded with his own "yes," the response of faith.

Almost all the available definitions of faith have been cast in the mold of essentialist philosophies. In the language of our own existential, personalist philosophies, I would like to define the act of faith as a "graced intuition." We are accustomed to distinguish between logical and intuitive minds, between reasoning and intuition. The logical type mind demands to see all the steps before it comes to the conclusion. Very often the intuitive mind will arrive at a truth without understanding just how it got there. Einstein, for example, said that he had intuited the theory of relativity long before he had logically worked it out. All of us, whether our minds are predominately logical or intuitive, have our moments of intuition. We know things that we cannot prove. One of the most delightful moments of human intuition comes when we realize suddenly that we are loved by someone else. Others can question us and cast their doubts about the reality of this love, but somehow and with certainty we know that we have been loved. We cannot logically reason to this certainty, but we know it nevertheless.

At the risk of offending male readers, I would like to compare the intuition by which we come to know God to the proverbial intuition of the female. It is not that I believe that women are endowed with a faculty not given to men. I rather think it is that women surrender more easily to the leadings of intuition than men, who more often feel adrift when they have lost the compass of strict logic and scientific verification.

Erik Erikson has speculated that women will open up whole new fields of enquiry in all the areas of research to which they are generally admitted. He believes that their intuitions will open up dimensions of truth that the masculine mind cannot conceive. Following this line of thought, he makes a most fascinating proposal. He suggests that, if our society is to become more and more computerized, then let the men build the computers, but let only women decide "what to ask and what not to ask the monsters, and when to trust them or not to trust them with vital decisions." The disinguished scientist, Lecomte du Nouy, in his book *Human Destiny,* contends that the sanest rational judgment is always questionable "because it is impossible to assemble all the elements required to give it an absolute value." The scientist, in other words, never has all the facts at hand. He will always operate on the basis of incomplete information. He must, of course, use his reason, "but he will perpetrate fewer errors if he listens to his heart," according to du Nouy.

In the graced intuition of faith, we are obviously drawn into new certainties by God who acts in us beyond scientifically provable facts. In making the act of faith we experience a deep sense of right order, of peace, and of meaning. We know: This is right. This is true. We have experienced the reality of a truth which we cannot logically prove.

As was said, the same thing is true in human love. We are told by those who have experienced the reality of loving and being loved, that there is a fulfillment that is possible only in a relationship of love. The lyricist calls it the "Sweet Mystery of Life." It is love and love alone that counts for anything. But it cannot be proved, and there are thousands of wilted people who cynically counter with: "Smoke Gets In Your Eyes." But those who have loved and been loved somehow know. They have experienced the reality of love, and it has led them out of themselves and into situations and responsibilities, even to heroic acts that the naked intellect would certainly call folly.

In the intuitions of faith and love, since they are not susceptible to intellectual analysis, the proof must be in the pudding. The only proofs for the realities of faith and love are those haunting people in our midst who have found faith and love, and who wear the smiles of fulfillment and who know the peace which we all seek. In matters of intuition there are no answers in the tables at the back of the book. Those who will not journey by night can only scratch their lonely heads and wonder.

It is very important to realize that this intuition of faith brings us primarily into contact with the person and love of God, and only secondarily into contact with a series of religious truths and commandments. While faith is ultimately an act of the intellect, it is also true that it is the acceptance of a person and the love of that person. This is what widens the dimensions of faith. As soon as we accept a person in the relationship of faith or love, every part of us is engaged in that act of acceptance. This was always the insistence of Jesus: Believe in *Me*! The fullness of his teachings or doctrines would be given only with the coming of the Holy Spirit.

> I do not pray only for them, but also for those who believe *in me* because of their message. (*John* 17:20)

> I have much more to tell you, but now it would be too much for you to bear. But when the Spirit of truth comes, he will lead you into all the truth. (*John* 16:12)

It is an historical tragedy that Christian preaching of God's word to be accepted in the act of faith has somehow inverted its priorities, stressing particular truths which Christianity has espoused rather than the person of its Lord, as the Apostles and early Christians did. It is not that Jesus did not have specific teachings, but these teachings will not make much sense to the person who has not first accepted Jesus himself.

God's ways are not our ways, and God's truth is often difficult for us. There is some pertinence here of the axiom that you can only know as much of another as you love. We have always said so glibly that love is blind. The real fact of the matter is that love is supersighted. Often we ask, with an adolescent naiveté, what so and so sees in his wife (or vice versa); he seems to love her so much. It is precisely because he does love her that he can know her in a way that is not available to anyone who does not love her. He sees things in her that only the eyes of love can see. So it is that only those who have been led over the unchartable course of faith to the threshold of God's love stand any chance of understanding him and his unique ways of dealing with man. We are not equipped to understand the truths of God—much less debate them—until we first understand the central truth of his person and of his love for us.

The relationship of faith

It is obvious that, if faith must be defined as an act, it must also be seen as an act that inaugurates a new relationship between God and the believer. In his external and internal words God has invited the believer-to-be into a relationship. In the act of faith, the believer responds to God: "I accept your invitation. I will be yours, and I want you to be mine." Two things should be said of the relationship that begins at this moment.

The first is that, as in all relationships, there are three distinct possibilities for its future. The believer can either grow in his relationship with God, or he can maintain a distant and superficial connection with God, or he can discontinue the relationship. The relationship of faith is subject to moments of crisis, turning points at which the believer can take the road either to danger or to opportunity, to a great depth or even to ultimate loss of faith. There are many different things that bring an influence to bear in this matter. The most important of these is the psychological balance of the believer and the environment in which he lives. However, more than anything else the destiny of this relationship will be determined by the amount of communication and interaction between God and his believer. There can be no doubt that all interpersonal relationships thrive on and are as good as the communication between the partners of the relationship. The communication between the inviting God and the accepting believer is the heart and meaning of faith, its life nourishment.

What is generally true of human relationships is also true of the relationship of faith; if it does not deepen, it will gradually die. Like the roots of a plant, faith must seek greater depth or be subject to the law of death. Interpersonal relationships are living things; their growth depends upon a dynamic evolution, new discoveries in the beloved and new self-revelations to the beloved. A relationship of love, St. Ignatius Loyola writes, consists in an exchange of gifts. Without these, a person cannot maintain interpersonal union. In the faith relationship, this interaction, this mutual self-relation, this exchange of gifts is largely dependent on what is called a life of prayer. If a person does not find God in prayer, he will not long retain a meaningful faith.

Secondly, crises in all relationships are inevitable and valuable when they are handled well. It is only through crises that the bonds of faith and love pass from an original fragility to a tested permanence. Through the growth that is possible in the successful handling of crises, faith becomes more and more marked by faithfulness and depth. It becomes the continued, personal response, the "yes" of man to the initiatives of God. But there are so many "yeses" inside the original "yes" of faith. Michel Quoist, in his book *Prayers,* writes:

I am afraid of saying "Yes," Lord.
Where will you take me?
I am afraid of drawing the longer straw,
I am afraid of signing my name to an unread agreement,
I am afraid of the "yes" that entails other "yeses."

Father Quoist says that "Only those who have experienced this 'wrestling' with God can really understand this prayer." While the relationship of faith transcends the usual avenues of human reason, it ruthlessly asks the adherence of the whole person and the commitment of his whole life. It is continually deepened and purified; it must have a history and an evolution of progress. It supposes continual departures from old stages of adherence to new ones. Like human love, it has its transformations. The tinsel of young faith, like the tinsel of young love, must gradually mature into gold.

Consequently, the relationship of faith is not without its pains and doubts. Those who are psychologically well integrated are usually spared the sharpest edges of doubt and pain in this matter. This is especially true if the family, educational, and emotional background of an individual are conducive to an integrated and balanced personality. Others, who never really "lose their faith," are spared the darkness of painful doubts and interior

115

conflicts, but only because they do not invest very much of themselves and of their lives in their faith. There isn't much for them to gain or to lose. However, such a person usually withdraws himself more and more from the influence and areas of grace, and gradually finds himself more and more distant from God. The deterioration of a meaningful faith is inevitable in this case.

The old axoim prevails here: You get what you give. In the begrudging believer, who never seems to catch fire or see his way clear to the self-donation involved in faith, faith can only deteriorate and die. There can be no resurrection into new life for those who are unwilling to die to themselves. As Jesus put it: "Unless the seed falls into the ground and dies, it cannot live. . . . The man who is always seeking himself will lose himself, but the man who is willing to lose himself will find himself." It is another application of the paradox of Assisi: "It is in giving that we receive."

CHAPTER FIVE

Religious Experience and Prayer

There is no scientific proof for the claims and contents of faith, nor is there any possibility of objectifying and substantiating any of the stages in the process of faith. The experience of coming into faith is simply not open to this kind of scientific investigation. No natural science could possibly establish as fact the supernatural entrance of God into human history or into an individual human life. These events lie outside the scope of the natural sciences. There is, however, what we might call an "existential" or experiential verification of faith. It is something like the experiential proof for the delight of chocolate ice cream or the beauty of a day in Autumn when the leaves are changing and the air is crisp. There are, in fact, many realities that can be known only through personal experience.

In the movie, *A Patch of Blue*, the blind girl asks her grandfather: "Old Paw, what's green like?" The irritated grandfather answers: "Green is green, Stupid. Now stop asking questions." There follows a pathetic scene in which the young girl paws the grass with her hand and rubs a leaf against her cheek, vainly trying to experience the reality of greenness.

The playwright, William Alfred, author of *Hogan's Goat,* once said: "People who tell me that there is no God are like a six year old saying that there is no such thing as passionate love. They just haven't experienced Him yet." The evangelist, Billy Graham, says: "I know that God exists because of my personal experience. I know that I know him. I have talked with him, and I have walked with him. He cares about me, and he acts in my every-day life." The experience of God must somehow be generally available because a recent Lou Harris poll revealed that 97% of the American people believe in some sort of a personal God. Statistics are not, and never could be, the last word. Faith remains a matter of personal experience, like chocolate ice cream, a day in Autumn, and greenness.

The whole presumption of Jesus seems to be that you and I can expect to experience in our lives the power, the peace, and the loving presence of God. In his last words to his Apostles before dying he says:

> I tell you the truth: whoever believes in me will do the works I do—yes, he will do even greater ones, because I am going to the Father. And I will do whatever you ask for in my name, so that the Father's glory will be shown through the Son. If you ask me for anything in my name, I will do it. If you love me, you will obey my command-ments. I will ask the Father, and he will give you another Helper, the Spirit of Truth, to stay with you forever. The world cannot receive him because it cannot see him or know him. But you know him, because he remains with you and lives in you. I will not leave you alone; I will come back to you. In a little while the world will see me no more, but you will see me; and because I live, you also will live. When that day comes, you will know that I am in my Father, and that you are in me, just as I am in you. (*John* 14:12-17)

Ultimately it is on this kind of interaction and experience that the relationship of faith thrives and deepens. This growth results from man praying and seeking God, and from God rewarding that effort by the touch of his hand on the life and person of the believer. Though some have tended to minimize the experience of God, depicting faith as a journey in total darkness looking for the light that comes only after death, I would like to take a strong exception to this. Limited though they may be in this life, we need and God is willing to provide moments of Thabor. It was on Mt. Thabor that Peter, James, and John saw for a brilliant moment the glory of God shining out of the person of Jesus. There must be transforming moments in the lives of each of us, when the light of God penetrates our darkness and the beauty of God delights our minds and hearts. Otherwise, faith would be the prescription for a very lonely existence.

Delusory and genuine religious experience

When I think of you reading the descriptions of religious experience that will follow, I can easily imagine your thoughts about some of the "religious" people you have known. There are always with us some withered and angry people who rain fire and brimstone on all those about them in the holy name of God and their faith. I think, therefore, that a word should be inserted here about the possibility of delusion and distortion in the matter of religious experience. There is, no doubt, a neurotic religious experience which must be distinguished from authentic experience of God. There are delusory or imagined religious experiences. Some of these pseudo-experiences, when reported, often produce only disgust in would-be believers.

Among such delusions, passed off as genuine religious experiences of faith, we might include the erroneous consciences of guilt-ridden people, whose experience of God seems to consist in a perpetual and terrorizing scrupulosity, a dehumanizing sense of sin and guilt. There are also other reported religious experiences that are in fact only thinly veiled forms of superstition. Such religiosity has been called "plastic-Jesus Christianity." The staple of such religious experience is to have a plastic Jesus riding on the dashboard of an automobile for protection.

There are many people, very likely, whose religious experience is a delusion. They range from nominal to devout believers, and the image of God for such people vacillates from that of a kindly old Santa Claus to that of a vengeful Scrooge who is trying to keep all of his books and all of his believers in order. In fact, much religious practice seems to be stifling and deadening. We all know some believers who multiply prayer forms, which have become meaningless after endless and boring repetition. They appear to take a pharisaical satisfaction in the belief that their works and prayers, by sheer dint of numbers, will save them. This seems suggestive of an obsessive-compulsive neurosis.

Most of us have also witnessed the apparent hypocrisy involved in hating one's neighbor with an accurate memory of his lapses, and yet never forgetting to bow one's head in grace before and after each meal. There are those, too, who give one hour and one dollar a week to God, and are complacent about their hopeful embezzlement of a place in heaven. Finally, though we could never exhaust the list of these pseudo-religious experiences, there is the legalistic mind of the person

120

who is afraid to make any of his own decisions, and consequently wants to follow minutely specified directions of someone else, while remaining in his own morality a perpetual child. Acts of conscience demand of us personal decisions and the willingness to live with our decisions. However, so many religious-type people seem to want to make no judgments and take no risks of their own.

We could go on giving instances and examples. Certainly you can think of many more than those described. However, it is extremely important to remember that, after all the repulsive and delusory religious experiences have been reported and catalogued, true religious experience remains not only a distinct possibility but an absolute need if one is to grow in the life or relationship of faith. Obviously, these genuine religious experiences will always be unique and individual. No two men will ever experience the reality of faith in precisely the same way. And so, although religious experience may be studied empirically, scientific explanations based on general laws will never be able to deal adequately with the unique experience of any given person.

However, there must be some criteria by which we can distinguish genuine from delusory religious experience. I would suggest that three tests may be applied. First there is the *time test*. Sometimes people in a moment of overcharged emotions report that they have felt the touch of God's hand. If such an experience is in reality only a natural force of emotion rising out of the circumstances of the moment, it will soon be spent and its effects will quickly disappear. However, if God has really entered the life of a man, he can never be the same again.

Secondly, there is the *reality test*. Delusory religious experience, invented to answer some subconscious need, such as feeling important or even the need to be punished, tends to isolate a person from the environment of reality. All delusion is a fantasy-wedge between the person and reality. Without going into a long disquisition about the meaning of contact with reality, it may suffice to say that each of us experiences a different degree of such contact. There are those who say a healthy *Amen* to life and there are those who spend an excessive amount of time in a fantasy world of daydreams. When God enters a human life, in an authentic religious experience, the result will be a deeper contact with reality. The recipient of such an experience of God will seem to be more alive, more aware of others and of the world about him. His perception of beauty will be keener, and his compassion for the suffering will be deeper.

Finally, there is the *charity test*. God, we have said, is love. He has made us to his image and likeness, and so our human vocation is to be loving. When God enters a human life, in whatever form or way and at whatever moment he chooses, the result will be that the person he touches will become more loving. Experiences that produce only complacency and self-righteousness cannot be from God. When a man truly invites God into himself and into his life, he can never be the same again, he will come into a deeper contact with the reality of his environment, and most beautiful of all, his heart will be gradually expanded with the highest of all God's gifts, the gift of love. St. Paul writes to the Corinthians:

> Set your hearts, then, on the more important gifts. Best of all, however, is the following way: I may be able to speak the languages of men and even of angels, but if I

have not love, my speech is no more than a noisy gong or a clanging bell. I may have the gift of inspired preaching; I might have all knowledge and understand all secrets; I may have all the faith needed to move mountains —but if I have not love, I am nothing. I may give away everything I have, and even give up my body to be burned—but if I have not love, it does me no good.

(I Corinthians 12:31—13:3)

The places of encounter with God

An authentic experience of God is possible for man. We can, if we seek it, experience his light when we are in darkness, his strength when we are weak, his presence when we are lonely, his healing when we have been hurt. In fact, the eyes of faith will seek and find God in all things. This was the specific religious genius of St. Ignatius Loyola, who gave his followers this rule: Let them seek and find God in all things.

We must seek and find God in the joys of human love, in the exhilaration of a sunset, starlight, a heavy snow bending the branches of evergreens in winter, in a fireplace at the end of a perfect day. All reality is a reflection of God, and God dwells, in a deeper mode of existence, in all things. There are many modes or strata of existence in all reality. The danger for us is the danger of superficiality. We might look at a beautiful bank of trees and see only lumber. We might look at a page of profound poetry and see only words. The deepest and the ultimate level of all existence is God himself, because all reality is a participation in his existence and in his beauty. Consequently, for the believer all reality becomes sacramental, a visible sign of the power and presence of God. The Jesuit poet, Gerard Manley Hopkins, writes in his poem "The Wreck of the Deutschland":

I kiss my hand
To the stars, lovely-asunder
Starlight, wafting him out of it; and
Glow, glory in thunder;
Kiss my hand to the dappled-with-damson west:
Since, tho' he is under the world's splendour and wonder,
His mystery must be instressed, stressed;
For I greet him the days I meet him,
and bless when I understand.

Hopkins is, in this quotation, expressing poetically the "encounter" with God in the world of nature. The believer does not just walk through this world, but he walks through God's world, the world which was made by God and which reflects his presence, the world in which he resides. In faith, the believer must somehow in his own way, according to his own abilities and temperament, encounter or experience the person of God in the daily affairs of his life, or it will be the gradual end of the life and relationship of faith. One German theologian of our day, Josef Pieper, says that the greatest obstacle to the life of faith is *inattention*. God is working, speaking, healing, restoring all around us; but we are blind men. We must pray with that blind man in the Gospels, Bar Timaeus, who sat outside the gates of the city, pleading: "Jesus, Son of David, have mercy on me. Lord, that I might see!"

Another great and saintly theologian of our day, Karl Rahner, lists a number of ways that the power of God and religious experience are open to us in our daily lives:

> ... cases where a spiritual experience of God seems credible: have we ever kept silent, despite the urge to defend ourselves, when we were being unfairly treated? Have we ever forgiven another although we gained nothing by it and our forgiveness was accepted as quite natural? Have we ever made a sacrifice without receiving any thanks or acknowledgment, without even feeling any

124

inward satisfaction? Have we ever decided to do a thing simply for the sake of conscience, knowing that we must bear sole responsibility for our decision without being able to explain it to anyone? Have we tried to act purely for love of God when no warmth sustained us, when our act seemed a leap in the dark, simply nonsensical? Were we ever good to someone without expecting a trace of gratitude and without the comfortable feeling of having been "unselfish"? If we can find such experiences in our lives, then we have already had that very experience of the Spirit which we are seeking.

(From *Do You Believe in God?*)

When the believer begins to look for and find God in all the things and persons about him, he develops what theologians call "Christian connaturality," an instinct born of grace that opens man to the power of God and attunes him to God's ways, which are so often different from our own. We are told that God is speaking to us in many times and in many places, but so often we perceive only absence and silence. These people, whom we call "saints"—they seem to hear him and see him everywhere and in everyone. Pierre Teilhard de Chardin, a man of extraordinary intelligence and bedrock faith, writes:

I see and touch God everywhere. Everything means both everything and nothing to me. Everything is God to me; everything is dust to me. Yes, Lord God, I believe . . . It is not just your gifts that I discern; it is you yourself that I encounter, you who cause me to share in your own being, and whose hands mold me.

(From *The Divine Milieu*)

Most of us seek the experience of the presence and power of God in matters that pertain to ourselves. In our congenital egocentric condition, we are always seeking God's favors for ourselves. We try to manipulate God's will to make our lives more pleasant and our persons more loved. We are always telling God what he can do for us, but to many of us it rarely occurs to ask God what we can do for him. Do we find God silent because we have not yet learned the first of his commandments, to love? Do we cry out for our own candy and cookies when so many of our brothers and sisters are combing through garbage cans to find the food to stay alive? God has a strange way of being silent to selfishness.

Perhaps we have not yet learned to seek first the kingdom of God and have the rest given to us. We have not learned to forget ourselves, and instead of trying to find our place in the kingdom of God we rather condescendingly try to fit God into our plans.

I think that this is the point of Malcolm Boyd's "Prayer of Discipleship," found in his book, *Are You Running With Me Jesus?* We try to dictate to God the manner of our witness and discipleship, instead of putting ourselves at his disposal. Maybe the experience of God, his power and presence are fatally prevented by our own incorrigible selfishness. Maybe we didn't hear Jesus say that the man who is always seeking his own life will never find it, but that the man who is willing to lose his life will find it. I personally think that there are many situations in my own life, situations in which I might have felt God's presence but didn't because my own presence was so preoccupying. I didn't hear God's requests of me because I was too busy forcing my requests on God. I got no answers because I was asking the wrong questions.

Somehow I feel sure that the most direct route to religious experience is to ask for the grace to give, to share, to console another, to bandage a hurting wound, to lift a fallen human spirit, to mend a quarrel, to search out a forgotten friend, to dismiss a suspicion and replace it with trust, to

126

encourage someone who has lost faith, to let someone who feels helpless do a favor for me, to keep a promise, to bury an old grudge, to reduce my demands on others, to fight for a principle, to express gratitude, to overcome a fear, to appreciate the beauty of nature, to tell someone I love him and then to tell him again.

There is a haunting possibility that I have not heard the voice of God speaking to me in all the circumstances and persons in my life because I have been asking the wrong questions, making the wrong requests. I have been too busy speaking to listen. The Psalmist prays: "Create in me, O God, a loving and listening heart!" Maybe I should pray for such a heart.

A long and slow process

We have been saying that the process of faith involves the careful reading of God's external word, the opening of the heart and mind to the interior word of God, which leads us to the act of faith. In turn, this act of faith introduces us into a new relationship of faith and this relationship is deepened by an ongoing religious experience, an interaction with God, an exchange of the gifts of love. At first this relationship is shallow and not a very real or deep thing, a fragile growth that must seek deeper roots. The poet Hopkins, whom we have already quoted, prays in one of his poems: "Thou Lord of Life, give my roots rain!"

One of the most discouraging aspects of man's search for God is the length and difficulty of the pursuit. Apparently God's face is not found on faltering feet. C. S. Lewis, in his book, *The Problem of Pain,* compares the process by which God transforms a human being through the life of faith to the domestication process of a dog. By nature a dog is wild, greedy, dirty, and undisciplined. We have to train him to live within a human family, to teach him a whole new set of signals and reactions. And, if the process is slow and painful to the trainer, it is an even deeper agony for the puppy, who doesn't see the serious criminality of chewing the sofa cushion or wetting the oriental rug.

The whole domestication process seems counter to his nature, but patience has its rewards and eventually there is effected a permanent elevation of his habits. In the end, he acts more like a human than a dog. He seems to be capable of affection; he is faithful, and even, in his own way, sociable. He seems to acquire the human qualities, the human traits that persevering training inculcates. It seems almost more natural for him to act like a human than like a dog. All the painful aspects of his training, especially the frightening and painful sessions in the tub of soap and water, are nothing compared to a new world of human enjoyments opened up to the little mongrel by human patience and sharing.

In a similar way, God's persevering efforts in us and in our lives have many painful moments, many baptisms of fire, sickness, loneliness, loss and failure, which we must pass through before we can enter into life, before a whole new world is opened up to us. There are moments when we feel just as miserable in the effort to be faithful to charity and prayer as the little puppy feels in the tub. We are often frightened and tremulous, and we really wonder and question what God is doing with us and our lives. Jesus encouraged us to be vigilant, to wait for the hour of God that will come and will be repeated in our lives. "Watch and pray," he said, "because no man knows the hour of God."

The loving hand of God is forever touching our lives, but there are special moments, the "hours of God," in which he touches us in a very special way and raises us to new heights of love, if we are open and willing. One of the English Jesuit martyrs, on the eve of his martyrdom, said that "the hour of God seems to come sometimes only at the limit of human endurance."

And that is why everyone should at some time in his life come to know a saint. There are saints among us, even though their names may never appear in our headlines or Missals. They seem to be living suggestions of what a persevering God can do in a faithful human being. It is strengthening for us to see the miracles that God has worked in them, the miracles of gentleness, faithfulness, unselfishness, innocence, joy, and peace. It seems more natural for them to act like God, who is love, than to act like men. The long and slow process of faith has transfigured them. They seem attuned to God in a way that makes most of us envious. They seem to speak his language, and he seems to speak theirs. They know his mind and heart and he knows theirs. As the French author, Leon Bloy, once said: "Only the saints are truly happy. The pity of our lives is that we are not all saints."

The length and difficulty of the process of faith through ongoing religious experience is aptly suggested in this quotation from Margery Williams' *The Velveteen Rabbit:*

> "What is REAL?" asked the Rabbit one day, when they were lying side by side near the nursery fender, before Nana came to tidy the room. "Does it mean having things that buzz inside you and a stick-out handle?"
>
> "Real isn't how you are made," said the Skin Horse. "It's a thing that happens to you. When a child loves you for

a long, long time, not just to play with, but REALLY loves you, then you become Real."

"It doesn't happen all at once," said the Skin Horse. "You become. It takes a long time. That's why it doesn't often happen to people who break easily, or have sharp edges, or who have to be carefully kept. Generally, by the time you are Real, most of your hair has been loved off, and your eyes drop out and you get loose in the joints and very shabby. But these things don't matter at all, because once you are Real you can't be ugly, except to people who don't understand."

Faith as a condition for religious experience

Most of us, in our desire for a meaningful faith, seem to be saying to God: "Show me, and I'll believe!" This approach never works. God has made it very clear to us, in the life and teachings of his Son, Jesus, that the process must be reversed. He is saying to us: "Believe in me, and I'll show you." Faith in him is an absolute prerequisite for the religious experience of God's power in and over our lives. Notice how many times in the New Testament Jesus tells the people who have received his favors that it was *their faith* that released his power. The Roman centurion is told that his son is cured "because of your faith" (*Matthew* 8:13). On the other hand, when the disciples come to Jesus to ask why they had been unable to cast the devil out of a certain young man, Jesus tells them very simply and bluntly:

> Your faith is too weak. I tell you this: if you have faith no bigger even than a mustard-seed, you will say to this mountain, "Move from here to there!" and it will move; nothing will prove impossible for you. (*Matthew* 17:20)

In the case of the paralyzed boy, who was lowered through the roof to be laid at the feet of Jesus, the Gospel simply says: "When Jesus saw their faith, he said to the paralyzed man, 'My son, your sins are forgiven. . . . I say to you, stand up, take your bed, and go home!" (Mark 2:5-12)

The classic example, however, is the woman troubled with hemorrhages for twelve years. She was the one who wanted merely to touch the hem of the garment of Jesus, believing that she would be cured. The example is classic because Jesus turned suddenly to his disciples, all of whom were caught in the crush of a great crowd, and asked a strange question: "Who touched my clothes?" The disciples were amazed: "You see the crowd pressing upon you and yet you ask, "Who touched me?" Finally the woman threw herself at his feet and told him the whole story. He knew someone had touched him in a special way because he had felt his healing power go out from him. He told her: "My daughter, your faith has cured you. Go in peace, free forever from this trouble" (Mark 5:24-35). Louis Evely describes the scene, in his book, *That Man Is You,* as follows:

> Now, everybody'd touched Him
>   everybody'd hustled Him;
>   still, nobody'd been cured or transformed.
> Only one had touched Him with faith;
>   and a profound sense of well-being coursed through her;
>   she was cured.
>
> As for us, we all read the Gospels now and then.
>   But if we approach them like an ordinary book,
>   they'll produce no extraordinary effect on us.
> We have to read them the way we'd have touched Christ—
>   with the same reverence,
>   the same faith,
>   the same expectancy.
>
> If someone eats the Eucharistic bread unwittingly—
>   say, a curious altar boy who tastes a host
>   without realizing that it's consecrated—
>   he doesn't commit a sacrilege,
>   but he doesn't receive Communion either.

131

He eats it like plain bread;
    and for him, it is:
        it doesn't bring him a particle of grace.
Well, that's how it is for the Gospels, too:
    read them without faith,
        and we read them without profit.

. . . . Let's test our faith on them,
    as that woman in the gospels tested hers on Christ.
    . . . . someday, we'll learn
        to listen as we should,
        to hear Him with faith
        to undestand Him as we're cured.

Certainly the surest, and perhaps the only, way to experience the power of God is to touch him with the expectant faith of this simple woman. Maybe the reason why so many of us find more evidence of the distance and silence of God than of his presence and power in our lives is actually the weakness of our own faith. St. Mark says that, in his own town, Jesus "could work no miracles there. . . . he was astonished at their lack of faith" (*Mark* 6:5-6).

For the sensual and faithless Herod, to whom Jesus was sent for judgment, he had only silence. The Gospel says that Herod "was greatly pleased; having heard about him, he had long been waiting to see him, and had been hoping to see some miracle performed by him. He questioned him at some length without getting any reply" (*Luke* 23: 8-9). Somehow those who do not believe find Jesus strangely silent to them.

The soldiers who crucified Jesus had their own version of the futile formula "Show me and I will believe." While he was dying on the cross, they called to him: "If you are really the King of the Jews, save yourself. . . . If we see him come down from the cross, we will believe." There was, of course, no answer to such a demand, only the silent echo of his own earlier prayer: "Father, forgive them, for they do not know what they are doing." I personally believe that this is the apropos theme that pervades the whole life and teaching of Jesus: *Believe first* and you shall certainly see the power of God! Do not come to me, asking to see signs and wonders so that you might believe. Believe in me first and I shall show you more signs and wonders than you could ever have expected. In fact, you will find yourself doing far greater things than I have done myself.

At this point there is room for an honest question and an honest answer. If a person finds himself with only a very weak faith, if he experiences more doubt than certainty within himself, what should he do? The answer I would give might seem simplistic or even repulsive to some, but here it is. One should read the New Testament slowly and prayerfully, trying to keep an open mind and an open heart. If it is true that God really takes and keeps the initiative in this matter of faith, it is up to him to act in us. Our only responsibility, since we cannot produce faith, is to be open to God. We must open our hearts to his gentle attraction and our minds to his illumination.

Jesus urges us to ask and to keep asking. Even for the non-believer, it would seem possible that he could read the Scriptures reflectively. He can invite Jesus into his mind and heart and into his life. And this is as far as man can go. The rest is up to God, who is always faithful and loving. For those in search of faith or deeper faith, some kind of prayer is an absolute essential. And so in the final section of this chapter, I would like to offer a basic suggestion about the manner and method of learning to pray.

The art of prayer: How to have a conversation with God

Prayer is a conversation or dialogue with God, and the art of prayer is knowing how to *speak to* and *listen to* God. If communication is to deepen the relationship of faith, the matter of this conversation cannot be superficial small-talk or even mind-talk. It must involve a total sharing or encounter of persons. When we pray we must open ourselves as deeply and honestly as we can; and we must be initiated into the delicate art of listening, as God opens himself to us.

Prayer has long remained an uncultivated art among Christians for two reasons, I suspect. The first is the invention of the printing press, which made possible the publication and distribution of prayer books. For too long now, Christians have been reciting words, composed by someone else, and have been encouraged to "say their prayers" by reciting these words over and over again. The success of such a prayer life is measured quantitatively, determined by whether one got all his prayers said before retiring for the night. Fortunately, this approach to prayer is losing its general appeal, but its disappearance has left a painful piety void as Christians search for new, more personal forms of prayer.

The second obstacle to a more meaningful prayer life among Christians is unfortunately not disappearing. It is not so much a theological position as an attitude or state of mind that does not expect God to be available to us in personal prayer. This prevalent "deistic" version of Christianity admits the existence of God, but describes him as inaccessible. No deeply personal relationship with such a God is possible. This attitude is religion without religious experience, faith without encounter, and a superficial relationship without the communication of prayer. Instead of finding the person of God in the world of creation, this attitude proposes that our only possibility is to find the world of creation itself, which is somehow vaguely identified with God.

In a recent book, *The Birth of God,* James Kavanaugh, the "modern priest" who looked over his shoulder at his "outdated Church," gives us a description of this posture. He identifies the new God he has found as the wind, rain, and sunshine. He contends that the best part of it all is that his new God". . . asks nothing of me." It is precisely this deistic influence in contemporary Christianity that many modern theologians and authors are trying to evict when they stress the possibility of encountering the unique, transcendent person of God in the world and in the personal dialogue of prayer.

Perhaps this kind of distant and bloodless relationship with God has resulted from the absence of spontaneous prayer in favor of prayer-book recitations. However, we might find another cause for modern deism in the traditional Christian presentation of God. In teaching and preaching, God was presented in terms of absolute majesty. From his throne, high and far above this world came decrees or commandments which institutional religion codified and expressed for him in legalistic formulations. Man was to work out his salvation in fear and trembling by obeying the will of God. In this presentation of God and his relationship with man, there is little or no room for personal encounter, for the requesting and asking, for the mutual self-disclosure and the self-donation which are the heart of the encounter that is prayer. God is an army officer barking commands to be obeyed blindly and instantly.

To understand prayer as communication in an interpersonal relationship, it will be helpful for us to notice how human beings come to know and love each other through communication. Love begins to grow when two people are willing to risk the real offering of self that can be achieved only in genuine self-disclosure. This is the moment when we really put ourselves on the line, in telling another who we really are, where we ache, and where we reside. Implied in this kind of communication is the obvious risk of rejection, but without the heart to take this risk there can be no real encounter. We give little or nothing of ourselves until we give ourselves in this way. Without it, the material and other gifts we exchange mean nothing. Love demands dynamic presence, not presents.

We put something of ourselves into the hands of another when we confront his freedom of choice to accept us or to reject us. The supreme risk, of course, is to tell another: "I love you." This usually implies a request of acceptance. Will you let me love you? Will you have me? This is what God has said to us, and it is hopefully what we will someday be able to say to God. But it may also be that, at this moment in our lives, much experience of true prayer lies between us and the ultimate commitment of ourselves to God in love.

First of all, how should we speak to God? Martin Luther, in his laws for successful prayer, gives as his first and foremost directive: *Don't lie to God!* At first, this might sound a little strange. After all, who can lie to God? But aren't we really lying when we say things we don't mean? Aren't we really lying when we use words to substitute for feelings we would like to have within us instead of using words which describe our actual feelings? Of course, we do this pious lying because we have been trained to believe that one should speak only reverently to God. When we read the prayers that others have written for us, or we compose our own versions based on the established protocol of dealing with God, when we say things like: "O Heavenly Father, I am filled with the deepest sentiments of faith, hope and charity . . ." we are, I think, lying to God. These are religious clichés. They express what we would like to think and feel, what we judge appropriate to think and feel. They do not express what we actually do think and feel.

In speaking to God, we must reveal our naked and true selves. We must tell God the truth, the truth of our thoughts, desires, and feelings, whatever they may be. They may not be what we would like them to be, but we must not fall into a trap; we cannot say to God what we would like the truth to be, but only what the truth actually is. The truth about ourselves may be frightening if we honestly face and reveal it. It may be, for example, that we are not really sure whether we believe or not. Certainly, if we are going to tell God who we are and where we live, all of us will have to tell him that something in us does believe and something else in us does not believe. We will have to tell him that we reside both in faith and in non-faith. We will have to pray: "Lord, I believe. Help my unbelief." It may be, too, that we find an anger or resentment for God and his ways of dealing with us. The only honest prayer at a moment like this is: "God, I am mad, damned mad."

Theorists of interpersonal relations urge us to ventilate our true feelings. Our thoughts may not be unique, original, or individuating; but our feelings always are. And there is the truth of our feelings that must be told in honest and authentic communication. This gut-level "telling it like it is" is the real gift of self. This is putting one's real self on the line. This is having enough trust in the greatness and understanding of God to tell him who we really are. It is the beginning of prayer.

I sometimes feel that the best examples of this type of prayer are to be found in the Old Testament. I hear Job cursing the day that God made him, Jeremiah accusing God of making a fool of him, and the Psalmist pleading with God to destroy his enemies; and I want to congratulate them for telling it like it was, for knowing how to pray.

Modern psychology, in a massive effort to release men from destructive, subconsciously repressed emotions, is trying through all sorts of therapeutic methods of sensitivity to put men in touch with their true feelings. The unwritten but practically certain promise is that, if one will learn to express his true feelings to others, he will in this communication deepen his relationships with others, and through these deepened relationships find mental and emotional health. This is equally true of prayer. If I mask myself before God, I will never really communicate with him, never really pray, never really get to know him, or feel that he knows me. The relationship of faith will be superficial at best, filled up with pious clichés, religious fantasies and delusions.

So I must open myself to God, but how does God open himself to me? Obviously, the thorniest problem of prayer is this, how God communicates himself to us. Most people who attempt the communication of prayer are willing to settle for a response of God that becomes clear only in the subsequent events of their lives. What happens to them after praying is God's response. To me this is very incomplete and unsatisfying, and I often wonder how such people actually go on praying, while waiting for delayed answers.

I would like to suggest that the fullness of real prayer includes a more immediate and direct response from God. But first, I want you to ask yourself these critical questions: Can God really communicate with us by putting new thoughts and new perspectives in our minds? Can he touch and calm our feelings, or actually say words to us? Can he reach our wills directly, by strengthening and encouraging us, by putting new desires in our hearts? Can God invade the store of memories in us, and stimulate helpful recollections? I think that only the person who believes in these possibilities is ready for a real two-way interpersonal encounter with God in prayer.

There are five faculties or antennae of reception in man that God can use to communicate with us. First, there is the *mind*. God can put new ideas directly into our minds. He can so illuminate our minds that we see him, ourselves, and the meaning of our lives more clearly. God can also touch our *wills* (hearts) by inspiring us with new desires, by giving us the courage to go on, by infusing into our wills the strength needed to rise above persistent habits of weakness. God can empower us, through this infusion of his grace into our wills, to love deeply and lastingly.

Besides these two supreme faculties of man, God can reach us through our *emotions* or feelings. When we are emotionally bitter or discouraged, when we feel the dull ache of loneliness, God can transform these emotions by the gentle touch of his loving power. God has effected not only physical cures in those open to him, but

139

emotional healings also. If God can make a leper clean, he can also make a neurotic normal.

We can also receive the impulse of God's grace in our *imaginations*. Under the stimulation of grace, we might see in our visual imagination a gentle glance of Jesus, or in our auditory imagination, hear him say: "I love you." In her trial for witchcraft, St. Joan of Arc maintained that she had been directed by the voice of God which she had heard within her. When one of the judges at her trial found this preposterous, and told her that she heard the voice of her own imagination, the uneducated little maid of Orleans agreed. She explained, however, that, if God really wanted to give her verbal directions, he would of course speak to her through her imagination. Granted that this might provide us with many difficult decisions about the genuinity of words heard in the imagination, the possibility that God can and the likelihood that God does communicate with us this way seems quite certain to most students and devotees of prayer.

The final channel of human reception is the *memory*. It is said that love consists in equal parts of memory and intuition. It is also said that the only real mistake is the one from which we learn nothing. When God communicates by stimulating in us a stored memory, he can stir up our love or prevent us from repeating an old mistake. In the ongoing relationship of faith, certainly the strongest support for most people is the remembered kindness of God.

Through these channels we have the possibility of direct and immediate communication from God. However, to open ourselves to these communications in fact and not just in theory, we must learn to open these channels to God. We must be introduced into the delicate and vanishing art of listening. This demands of us a willingness to sit quietly at the feet of God, in his personal, dynamic presence. We must be willing to shut out all the noises and distractions of the scene about us, and in the stillness of a living faith, to await the touch of God.

You will pardon, I hope, a word of personal testimony. I have prayed this way for some time and with a rewarding regularity felt the touch of God, slowly straightening out the tangled perspectives of my mind, helping me to see the important things in life and giving me the ability to distinguish them from the unimportant; rekindling in me the desire to love and help others, even when there was no emotional return or reassurance of gratitude; pacifying my feelings in moments of discouragement and anger. I have felt the touch of his grace in my imagination; I have heard him say: "I love you. I am with you. I am counting on you." And many times he has revived in me memories of his tenderness, strengthening me for the future by reminding me of his faithful help in the past.

I have asked others to attempt this approach to prayer for a period of time, and requested that, if they experienced only silence and absence, they should let me know, even by an anonymous note. I am being honest when I tell you that no failures have ever been reported, although I am sure that many did not try the experiment of prayer as suggested. But I have come to believe that God is there for those who seek him.

Through this kind of interaction and dialogue with God, we gradually come to know both God and ourselves. Even though we start the search for God with massive false impressions of who he is and what he thinks of us, this kind of prayer will gradually bring us to a clearer and truer image of God, just as surely as human communication gradually has brought us to know those other humans whom we love.

We do not need a proper and accurate portrait of God before the dialogue of prayer can begin. If this were the case, none of us could ever pray. Getting to know God, or anyone else, is a dialectical process. It involves learning by making mistakes, by correcting old impressions, by gaining new insights. Being wrong about who God is doesn't mean that we haven't really been talking to him. Prayer is essentially encountering God and through these encounters getting to know him.

Prayer, then, requires the willingness in us to "level" with God, with all the assurance of two people who are really committed in love to each other. If we try to silence or suppress rebellious, negative emotions, our relationship with God may be tranquil but it will also be distant and cold. Prayer also requires of us a willingness and ability to listen, with all of our faculties. We must learn to be receptive, passive to the touch of God. The deadliest delusion would be to approach prayer with the idea that God doesn't have anything to say to us, or that he won't. Who could go on talking to a wall?

What we need most of all, I suspect, is the experience of success at prayer. Once we have truly opened to God, with no clutched, concealing hands behind our backs, and once God has touched us in the depths of our being, we can never be the same again, and he can never seem the same again.

CHAPTER SIX

The Struggles and Stages of Faith

Becoming a believer is a process, just as learning to love is a process. Both involve interpersonal relationships. Both imply moments of crisis, ups and downs, progression and regression. Success is not assured in either process. The child trying to bid farewell to his "infantile id" of self-centeredness may never learn to relate in love to others. The believer may never arrive at the surrender of a deeply personal faith. At stake in the process of faith is man's relationship with God. Most of us tend to misconstrue faith as an act of acceptance or rejection of various religious doctrines. The fact is that the heart of faith is really an I-Thou encounter and relationship. The revelation of God which we accept in the act of faith is not so much a series of intellectual propositions demanding an intellectual "Amen" from us, but rather a living portrait of a living person extending to man the hands of love and asking a total human response. This response is man's faith.

To become a believer is only a beginning because faith is a living relationship, and living things are susceptible to growth. We cannot psychologize or program the grace of God who waters this growth in his own mysterious ways and at his own mysterious times. Faith is God's work, and in this sense faith is always enclosed in profound mystery. But faith also has a human side. Grace builds on and in human nature. It is born in man by God's action, but it usually develops according to certain laws as man himself develops. Consequently, it is possible to investigate the human experience of faith and its normal development in man. Just as being a person involves the constant process of becoming a person, so being a believer implies becoming a believer.

Recently I saw a button, on the lapel of a friend, which read: PBPWM — GINF — WMY. The wearer explained that it meant: "Please be patient with me. God is not finished with me yet." Faith is indeed God's production in man, but his work requires human cooperation and human cooperation depends upon many things: time, age, temperament, environment, strength and weakness of personality, and psychological maturity. God works in men as he finds them. Consequently, the process of being-becoming a believer has a human history of stages and struggles.

The two critical concepts involved in faith

From a human viewpoint, the success or failure of the faith process will be controlled by two critical concepts more than by anything else. They are one's concept of God and one's concept of himself (his self-image).

It is obvious that our human, interpersonal relationships are constantly threatened by personal insecurity. Personal insecurity, from whatever source, finds it very hard to trust in love, even when love seems to be offered to us. Because we are insecure

144

about ourselves, constantly questioning our own loveability, we tend to put offered love through a hundred tests. We want to be sure that this love is really durable. We want to know: "Are you really going to love me as I am, or is this just a pretense?" It is only when another's love and acceptance has been certified as true that we can take off our masks and come out, inch by inch, into the revitalizing atmosphere of trust and faith.

Of the two critical concepts, some primacy of importance must be given to the concept of God. It is only through the concept of the one who loves us that our own self-concept can be altered, so our maturation in faith depends largely on who we think this God is who has invited us into the relationship of faith. If only we could be sure that God would be patient, gentle, and understanding with us.

In our human condition of insecurity, we are always looking for someone who isn't hard on others, someone who is not judgmental and severe in his thinking of others. We listen to those around us in search for such a person, to see what they say, to test their compassion for human weakness. We want to be sure before we run the risk of self-revelation and self-donation. We ask ourselves if this or that person is self-righteous, one who leaves no margins for error, one with whom no secret or sensitivity is safe. We are constantly reading the signs that others send out, and we are either threatened or reassured by what we see. If the signs are not favorable, we readjust our masks and seek the safety of distance. We are not about to leap into such frigid and frightening waters. We refuse to expose anything of our true, vulnerable selves. If only we could believe that God truly is love.

All human beings are, to some extent, afflicted with a sense of inadequacy and ugliness. We are afraid to venture out of ourselves into a relationship if we feel that the price will be a further expose of our inadequacies and ugliness. This is the tyranny of a bad self-image. Only someone that we can trust utterly can free us from these shackles of self-doubt. One of the laws under which we humans must live and struggle is this, that we cannot really know who we are until we have let another know us and accept us for what we are.

Consequently, in the process of faith, we must somehow learn to break the fixation we have with questioning ourselves, and turn to the more profitable question: "Who are you, O my God?" It is only under the gentle reassurance of his grace that we can know he really accepts and loves us, that he is understanding of our failures. And only then can we finally understand, accept, and be comfortable with ourselves. The question "Who am I?" leads inward, and few answers are to be found there. The other question "Who are you, O my God?" leads outward, and this is the direction of human salvation.

When our own personal doubts and insecurities have been calmed in the gentle presence of God, through the I-Thou encounter of faith, we can then experience a mysteriously new sense of identity and fulfillment. The interior cleavage that divides us will then begin to heal, and the war that rages inside us will then be ended in a surrender of trust. The million doubts that shred and destroy peace in the heart of man will then begin to settle like particles of dust that rise over the field of battle; and the pieces of the antagonizing jig-saw puzzle of life will begin to fall into place. Who are you, O my God? I really need to know.

What all this means is that, in the process of faith, our greatest need is constantly to revise our concept of God, who is always infinitely greater and more loving than our finite minds can possibly grasp. And so, we must be willing to study God in his own word of revelation, especially as he has made himself known to us in the humanity of Jesus. No, at second thought, not just study. We must have new and living experiences of, encounters with God. We must get to know him from first hand experience. We must pray. We must dialogue with God, telling him as honestly as we can who we are, and turning over to him the faculties of human perception to let him tell us who he is.

Many of us have studied God. We have memorized answers in catechism classes, in theology seminars. And from all this we have been left as barren, lonely, and isolated as when we started our study. This kind of purely intellectual digestion can be a surprisingly sterile process. What we really need is the type of encounter that will penetrate and involve every part of us. Man knows with his whole being what the mind alone can never grasp. The fact is: we need to know God's presence and feel loved by him. We do not need to know *about* God, but to know *him*. We foolishly keep protesting that we are intellectuals, and we engage in a great deal of God-talk. But the understanding of God and the human identity which this understanding alone can confer is a matter of the marrow of the bones, air in the lungs, and blood in the veins.

Doubt and crises of faith

For the word *crisis,* the Chinese use a combination of two characters. These two characters are those which designate "danger" and "opportunity." This disjunction seems to be true of every crisis. It is a turning point, and, depending on how one makes the turn, he can find danger or opportunity. The

147

forks in the road of human life that demand decisions of us are always crossroads of danger and opportunity. As in the medical usage of this term, when a patient is pronounced "critical," the implication is that he can move either towards life or death.

In the process of faith, doubts and crises must occur. Paul Tillich points out that only through crises can faith mature. Doubt eats away the old relationship with God, but only so that a new one may be born. The same thing is true of our human, interpersonal relationships. They grow from initial fragility into permanence only through the tests of doubt and crisis. So Kahlil Gibran says that we can "forget those we have laughed with, but we can never forget those we have cried with."

There is something in older people that feels uneasy with, or even resents, crises of faith in the young. We lose sight of the fact that faith can mature only because of these crises. We forget that no one can say a meaningful "yes" of commitment until he has faced the alternate possibility of saying "no." The most destructive thing we can do to those passing through periods of crisis is to attempt to silence these legitimate doubts and encourage their repression. Repressed doubts have a high rate of resurrection, and doubts that are plowed under will only grow new roots. One thing is certain, that passage through the darkness of doubts and crises, however painful they may be, is essential to growth in the process of faith.

Faith and infancy

A noted preacher was once asked by an admirer how long it took him to prepare one of his sermons. The preacher replied: "All my life." Our yesterdays lie heavily upon our todays, and our to-days lie heavily upon our tomorrows. All of our lives we are being shaped and we are shaping ourselves for the present moment; and in each present moment all that has been done to us and all that we have done rises to the surface. It is this life experience, even from the very beginning of life, that conditions our reaction to the crises that confront us. There is very little in any human life that does not bring its weight of influence on the moment when man meets God, very little that does not condition the ability of man to believe in and relate to God as I to Thou.

The human vessel that is capable of holding the grace of faith is shaped by a long process. It is quite clear that human stability lies as a foundation to the edifice of faith. In each period of human growth, there seem to be certain normal developments, perceptions and perfections, which enrich the humanity of man and provide an essential element for true and mature religious faith.

It might at first seem strange that experiences in infancy should have any bearing on the faith process in a human being, but psychologists are more and more certain that the first years of life are the most important. It is beyond question that one's emotional stability and personal identity are most influenced by the first several years of life. Psychologist Henri Nouwen points out that three steps taken in the first five years of life, to the extent that they are achieved, provide a very important and essential human constituent of true religious faith.

The first of these steps is the discovery of *otherness*. In the first two years of life an infant discovers, to his considerable frustration, that he is not the only existent being. He is not the center of the universe. It has been said that man is born with clenched fists, in the gesture of possession, but that he dies with open, surrendering hands in the gesture of dispossessing the world. To the infant, after birth, his mother is an extended part of himself. She is the smiling face that appears when he cries, the comforting hands that alleviate his uncomfortable feelings. He thinks that his wailing creates her milk, that his cry produces her presence. He somehow concludes that his needs evoke their own satisfaction. The stage is set for the first of life's great discoveries: otherness.

Gradually during infancy, the baby discovers that mother is not a part of himself but another, distinct person. He discovers that he does not rule the world by his whims and whimpers. There are other persons, events, and things in the world which are distinct from himself. Of course this discovery in infancy is only partial. Even as adults, most of us seem to have given only a superficial consent to the fact of otherness. We are tempted to be so preoccupied with ourselves that we think of others only as relatively distinct from ourselves. We pay lip service to their autonomy, but somehow we continue to consider them as extensions of ourselves, to be manipulated according to our needs. Success in mastering the fact of otherness admits of various degrees.

Obviously, true faith can be only as sound, realistic, and objective as is our acceptance of otherness. The less complete the discovery, the more we will be tempted to accept an infantile version of faith that is largely the wishful thinking of a child. The person who has not digested and mastered the fact of otherness will tend to treat God as a part of himself, a Daddy or Mommy who appears whenever he cries out in pain, whose very presence is evoked by his own needs, by his illness, failure, grief, or insecurity.

The second momentous discovery of infancy is the formation of *language*. Between the eighteenth month and the third year of life, unintelligible sounds become words, and words begin to fall into groups that sound something like sentences. It is a comforting discovery for the infant, who has just surrendered his sovereignty over the world. He finds in this new discovery of words a mysterious power over the things that he had to surrender in his confrontation with otherness. Now he can just keep saying "Ice cream . . . Ice cream . . . !" and behold, ice cream appears.

The discovery of language that is of importance to the development of faith is not the discovery of how to manipulate reality by commanding things or using words to substitute for inner realities. The infant must come to realize his words do not always produce what he desires, and that they are really not a substitute for his inner dispositions. "Me nice boy . . .," after a minor naughtiness, may bring him a swift pat on the bottom, and the school of human discovery is in session again. The authentic discovery of language is the realization that language is a means of true self-communication.

This discovery of language may, like the discovery of otherness, be more or less imperfect. We may continue all our lives to concede only a partial admission of the facts. And whatever limitations we suffer in this matter will condition the authenticity of religious faith. Faith and religion are, like most human realities, filled with words. There are not only the words of prayers, litanies, and invocations, but the words of dogmatic formulas, liturgies, novenas, grace before and after meals.

The discovery of language is complete only when we realize the true nature of words, namely to express to others our true inner reality. The danger of imperfect realization is this, that we are tempted to think that we can summon God out of oblivion, the way we call an old friend for whom we have found sudden need or use. We are tempted to use words as a substitute for inner realities, the way we do in so many discussions. We complain vocally about social injustices, and we feel comforted after making lyrical statements on the subject. But it may be that our real indignation is only about two syllables deep. We talk but we do nothing. We have substituted words for real feelings and deeds.

We can also make acts of humility, somehow believing that the words are facts. We can say nice, wordy prayers and make beautiful speeches to God without being willing to sacrifice anything of ourselves in order to make those words reality. We can superstitiously think that these words exercise some sort of mastery over our gods, our devils, our inner dispositions and choices. We can think of our words as omnipotent utensils to manipulate reality. If we do not outgrow this superstition, adult faith is not very likely.

The final step in the human evolution of infancy that confers authenticity and maturity upon religious faith is the *formation of conscience*. This takes place between the third and fifth years of human growth. To the extent that we have mastered the realization of otherness and the meaning of language, we are challenged by this even more important step which leads us from external regulation of our conduct to inner realization. During the first three years of life, mother and father are external agents of discipline. Things which they say are wrong, are wrong, and simply because they have said so. They sanction their judgments with occasional rewards or punishment.

Between ages three and five, the external agents of discipline should yield to inner convictions, the first inner realizations of morality. The formation of conscience is achieved in the process that we call interiorization. Gradually we come to recognize the objective value of certain judgments, standards, ways of acting. We begin to see why we shouldn't pick flowers from a neighbor's garden or hit our little sisters. Formerly these judgments were reinforced by parental sanction. In this first stage of moral enlightenment, the reasonability of certain conduct becomes an inner realization. Conscience, in spite of a well-circulated rumor, is not a little voice inside of us. It is a practical, moral judgment about the rightness or wrongness of given actions. To the extent that one learns to make his own judgments of this kind, he has taken the third step towards maturity and towards the possibility of a real and authentic faith.

Needless to say, this step is subject to the same possibilities of incompletion that the others are. We can fail to interiorize, to accept values for our own. We can grow up respecting only external policemen. We will be honest only as long as they are watching. We will be righteous only when there is a good probability that we would be caught in doing wrong. On a more subtle level, we will seek to find some external source of direction who will accept the responsibility for our decisions and our actions.

Many supposedly mature believers have been educated to ask a priest or clergyman to make their decisions. They follow his advice. They develop what has been called a purely "external" conscience, but it is really no conscience at all, since there is no inner evaluation of ideals, no personal deliberation of circumstances, no judgment by the lights of the moment. The immediate rewards of having others make our decisions is obvious, but if one does not want to take any responsibilities in life for his own judgments and actions, he will simply never grow up. The ability to make one's own judgments and take the responsibility for one's own decisions is a necessary part of the maturation process, and an exercise that is vital to committed faith.

Failure to develop one's own conscience by the process of interiorization can result in the prolongation of infantile dependency. The person who will not make his own decisions and choices will never relate maturely to God because he will always want God to be a "Big Daddy" who takes care of him. Freud has suggested in his *Future of an Illusion* that religion thrives because it offers men who are really children a continuation of the infantile life, lived securely in the arms of a loving, omnipotent, omniscient father. God, says Freud, is the projection and prolongation of the ever present desire for shelter, protection, and security. Such a temptation is no doubt possible.

God himself is no substitute for conscience. Things are good or bad, actions are right or wrong, because they are such in themselves, not because of a declaration by God. A person who relates to the God who stands as a substitute for conscience has nothing to decide or judge for himself. He simply has to ask God to make his decisions for him. What we are saying in no way undermines the very profitable practice of "praying for light." God can give his illumination to the mind of man, and it is a part of wisdom and faith to seek this light.

It is a safeguard against our tendency to "rational-ize." However, what God will show us is the objectivity of things, so that we can come to our own right judgment. If God preempted all our decisions and judgments, he would be contributing to the delinquency of minors by treating us as perpetual children.

Faith in childhood: The crisis of growth

The highest hurdle that must be cleared on the way to mature faith is always the same: selfishness. The inexorable law is that to go out to another in love and faith we must necessarily leave ourselves. An understandable self-centeredness is the hallmark of childhood. At first the child thinks of God as a super life-size version of his earthly father. The first prayer that most Christian children learn to say is the "Our Father." What the child imagines is really his own father, somehow bigger and better but basically the same. Because of the obvious limitations he experiences, the child's relationship with his father is one of almost total dependence. Consequently, the protective love of God is just about as real to him as the human love and concern shown to him by his earthly father.

It is not surprising, then, that the child's relationship with God is also one of almost total dependence. It is a child's version of faith, characterized by constant asking, but the child is capable of no more. Almost all of the prayers of a child are prayers of petition. His faith, in so far as it is conscious, is largely the result of his environment. In fact, his faith is really not very much of his own, but is usually only an echo of the faith of his parents and those who are molding his person and life. Someday, he will have to make this faith fully his own, but the process will involve many years of painful crises and doubt. In fact, doubt will consume his old concepts of God and even the very foundation of his old way of relating to God, but these are the growing pains of faith.

The depth and beauty of a child's faith is God's secret. While his faith is modeled on the faith of his parents, it does in fact have its own genuineness. It is a fragile but real beginning. Everything that grows is fragile and shallow in the beginning. Just as the human body begins slowly to grow and take shape, so the faith of the child has its own real but undeveloped beginnings. The rapidly changing emotions and thoughts of a child do not make for depth, but they do not deny the existence of all real faith. The child can, in his own way, relate to God just as really as he can relate to his parents and playmates. And God will deal with him with the same tolerant understanding and allowance which parents should practice.

Having experienced the first glimmerings of conscience, the concept of human freedom is a new experience to the child. The seventh and eighth years are usually years of continued subjectivity and self-centeredness, but the child will begin to feel the impact of his own choices. He will experience the need to be loved, helped, encouraged and forgiven; and these are all new depths of his original discovery of otherness. At age eight or nine, he will gradually show the first signs of emergence from this subjectivity and almost absolute self-centeredness. His incipient relationship with God will make its first demands on him. Acts of offering will slowly introduce themselves into his prayers of asking.

From ages nine to twelve, the God who makes requests will enter his life; and a sense of fidelity or infidelity will become a reality to him. It is very important that, at this time, his instruction be both human and sound. To present an over-demanding, or worse a threatening, God to a child of this age is to invite either scrupulosity or in the end rebellion.

The faith crisis during these ages, from five to twelve, is the challenge of growth. When a child first enters school, almost everything he thinks is only what he has heard in the protective environment of his own home. Expression of faith in him is a memorized recitation of what he has heard. In these school years, he begins to learn things his mother and father might not know, like the new math, historical and scientific facts. The first time he stumps his mother or father, or proves to know something that they don't, he is at the threshold of a new kind of existence: his own.

Having fought the battles and endured the traumas of disillusion in infancy, the most critical stage of human development, he has now been ripped from his mother's arms and the sweet security of home, and thrust into a new atmosphere. The first great human experiences of life have all taken place in the home from which he has ventured forth. There he hopefully experienced trust, love, concern, and happiness. All the adjustments he had to make in the first five years of life were made in the security of his own family and home. Some sort of personality structure and balance were established there, and now they are to be put to the test of the school years. Here, in his new environment, the major patterns of conduct have to undergo some sort of adjustment. They will be confirmed or changed, enlarged or diminished, retained or relinquished. It is his first experience with a peer-group.

The one area of life that is usually not much affected by this larger world and peer-group is that of religion. It customarily remains a "private affair." Whatever religious attitudes or practices had evolved in the first five years of life usually remain pretty much the same. No new adjustments are needed. Religion can easily be allowed to remain a static and separate reality in his life. Unless he runs into an informed and dynamic instructor in religion, there isn't likely to be a "new faith" in the sense that there is a "new math." And this is precisely the hazard of faith in these years: there may be no new intake of experience. The prayers he says, the Masses he attends may be the same familiar rituals. There will be new ways of learning to read and other pedagogical innovations, but his parents and most of his teachers will not allow any tampering with his original religious formation. God will not get a new face.

The danger is that most people, having no new intake and feeling no outside pressures, tend to cling to a child's formulation of faith and religion. The same practices, attitudes, and concepts of religion can unfortunately endure for a lifetime, if they are found to be consoling. The famous psychologist, Gordon Allport, in his book, *The Individual and His Religion*, suggests that this kind of stagnation is the greatest danger in early religious formation.

Maturing in faith is possible only if faith is integrated into the whole framework of life. All new knowledge and experience should somehow expand one's religious frame of reference and concepts. A child's faith is largely not his own, and, if religion and faith are kept encapsulated in routine rituals and rubrics, the result will be that faith and religion will wear thin, become meaningless and lose all relevance. After a while, use of the sacraments will get to be a "drag," and there will follow long intervals of disuse. For growth in faith, it is essential that we maintain some flexibility, that we possess some willingness and desire to integrate new insights and revise old positions. The danger is atrophy; and, when atrophy sets in, apathy is not far away.

Faith in adolescence:
The crisis of self-acceptance

In early adolescence, approximately from age twelve to fourteen, young people are distracted from the invitation of faith by the strong appeal they find in themselves to break away from childhood, to become adults and to take part in the world around them. There is a temporary return to subjectivity and egocentrism at this time. The first attempts of the young adolescent to join the dance of life are usually awkward and ineffectual. He seeks to become a full-fledged member of his peer society, to which he is inclined to conform, and whose codes he scrupulously copies. The survival of faith at this age usually depends strongly on the image of God which he has inherited from his childhood teaching. It is extremely crucial at this period that he can think of God as an ally, as someone who is on his side, who has understood and loved him as he is. Many children are given an image of God with which they cannot comfortably live, an image that is definitely not viable in the stormy period of adolescence.

Middle adolescence covers the fifteenth to the eighteenth year. The preoccupation of the young person at this time is the restless tension he experiences between his *gregarious instinct,* which propels him to become a part and carbon copy of his peer group, and his instinct for *individuation,* which urges him to seek his own identity and not to be lost in the large sea of humanity. He wants to belong to a group, and at the same time he wants to do his thing, regardless of what others might think or do or try to impose on him. Consequently, a certain amount of rebellion against parents and a definite inclination to the jargon and styles of the peer group is quite normal at this time.

Within himself the youngster in middle adolescense experiences the fright of a thousand doubts about himself. The features of his face and the contours of his body begin to develop, and he wonders what he will look like when the process is completed. He wonders if he will be successful in his relationships with those of the opposite sex, to whom he feels a new attraction. He wonders if his talents, athletic, intellectual, and social, will be adequate to gain for him some personal distinction. He is going through the so-called identity crisis. And his ability to open to the invitation of God is greatly limited by these other preoccupations. Having to deal with the crises of identity and sexuality, he is left very little energy or inclination to go outside himself and to find meaning in a relationship with God. He needs all the help he can get to achieve the Copernican revolution that will slowly turn the focus of his attention from inward to outward, from self to others.

If infancy is the most important stage in human development, adolescence must certainly be the second most critical stage. It is a time of dramatic changes, psychological as well as physical. Life outside becomes suddenly more complicated, with classroom competition, the social scramble, athletics and acne. But the turbulence of life outside is nothing compared to the reverberations inside. The adolescent usually feels within himself like a stranger in someone else's house. The ambivalence of adolescent emotions is particularly puzzling and frightening to him. He can love and hate the same person almost simultaneously. He can want to live and die, to give and take, to help and hurt, to get close to others and to run away from them, all at the same time.

The strongest drive is to get out of childhood, and the symbol of this successful emergence is an affected estrangement from his parents. It is his only way to assert individuality. The adolescent is terribly self-conscious; in fact, he lives in an "I-centered" world.

The great crisis of adolescence, with regard to faith, is the crisis of self-acceptance. The test is whether an individual can understand and accept the human condition of weakness and ambivalence. We are all creatures of weakness in strength and strength in weakness; we are fractions, creatures of ambiguity. There is no action so bad that there is not some good mixed up in it, and no action so good that it does not contain an alloy of selfishness. We are creatures of ups and downs, agonies and ecstasies, of strength and weakness. We bounce back and forth, like ping-pong balls, between altruism and selfishness. It is precisely this discovery of the human condition that often puzzles and demoralizes the adolescent.

While the adolescent is experiencing all these dissonant sounds inside him, it is important that he does not hear religion offering him only criticism. A relatively recent study indicated that many adolescents give up on religion, not because of a direct rejection, but because they feel it is an impossible ideal. A preachy and prohibitive type religion will condemn all the very things that he is feeling inside, the things he feels impelled to do. Self-righteous preachers of the Gospel, which doesn't sound like "good news" to him, tell the adolescent that he should never become angry, should never curse, gossip, steal, masturbate, or become sexually curious. It is irritating to be constantly subjected to this shame, to have to listen to a continual reprehension by religion.

Furthermore, religion seems to be promoting sterling products like love, kindness, obedience, and purity in such a high key hard-sell that the attainment of these virtues as they are preached seems hopelessly distant and impossible. It is the lonesome tunnel of adolescence, and he is crawling through it on bleeding hands and knees. He is troubled by a double darkness, the conviction that his experience is unique and the certainty that no one can really understand.

There are two urgent needs for the young person going through this trial. The first is someone who understands him and accepts him with all of his vacillation and ambivalence. There can be no doubt that each of us needs to be understood and accepted by another before we can understand and accept ourselves. The adolescent feels an almost compulsive need for this kind of understanding, for someone who will listen to him, take him seriously, and accept him for what he is. The second need is for a model. While things are in such a state of flux inside and around him, he needs very badly to see someone who has passed through this wilderness, who has passed out of the darkness into the light, who has emerged from the turbulence which he is experiencing into serenity. He needs a model of faith. He needs someone he can admire, someone he would want to "turn out like," who stands firm and peaceful in his faith.

But the people outside, and especially those he would like most to have as his models, often seem to be saying to him, "Don't rock my boat, Kid. . . . You think you've got problems. Wait tell you grow up. You're only a punk." Inside, there is a restive feeling of hypocrisy, a disquieting feeling that no one could ever love him if they knew him as he really is.

The "rah, rah, over the top, boys!" exhortations of religion can seem very oppressive and unreal at this time. All that faith and religion honor seem so far away from him, so negative and disintegrating. He feels that he could never be what religion asks of its believers. There is a strong temptation just to give it all up. He is comforted by the fact that a lot of other people have already given it up. There is some kind of safety in their numbers. Operating on this logic, some make a clean and quick break. Others suffer from gradual alienation, and slowly fall away.

Sometimes parents or teachers directly or indirectly suggest to young people another way of handling this turmoil and these doubts. It is perhaps the most dangerous of all solutions. It is the alternative of submerging all these doubts, to become a conformist. This is the denial of "repression," and it asks that one simply deny the very existence of any doubt or any unchristian urges in emotions or body. The young person in question must keep reminding himself that he is all the things religion prizes, insisting that he never feels anything that is religiously undesirable. He becomes a little rigid and tense, a little spooky, and anything but human.

The attitude of repression blocks the growth of authentic faith. Denying the reality of the human condition is the equivalent of playing a role, wearing a mask. The mask in this case may look angelic, but it is a wall of unreality between man and God. It sabotages all possibility of real communication and all honest dialogue with God. It is a matter of going through treadmill motions to the stage directions of a grade-school catechism. Honest self-acceptance of and adjustment to the human condition is an absolutely essential condition for the maturation of faith. Rebellion and repression are the alternatives of immaturity, dead-end streets, and death warrants for true peace and happiness. Only the honest admission of all that we are, the honest self-acceptance of the human condition, can bring men true peace and set them on the course to mature faith.

Faith in early adulthood:
The art of risk and revision

Of all the various times of crisis in the process of faith the definitive time is between ages eighteen and twenty-five. This has been called the "age of conversion." The Latin verb *vertere,* from which our word "conversion" is derived, means to "turn to," and the question is: Will this young adult turn from himself and his own egotistical concerns to others and to God? The capacity of a young adult to encounter God will, of course, depend heavily on his maturation as a human being. If he remains deeply immersed in himself and barricaded by his masks and facades of self-protection, true encounter with God or, in fact, with anyone will be very unlikely.

To lay one's self on the line rather than put one's

act on the stage, to trust the acceptance and love of another, is to run the risk of ridicule or rejection. To listen to another openly, which is vital to both the human and divine encounters, is to run the risk of letting another change us. We are reluctant to let anyone else unknot our prejudices, or revise our delicately balanced personality structures. We resist the surrender required in true relationships, because intimacy and openness threaten us.

The college years have been called the "age between homes," between the parental home and the hoped-for home of one's own. In college there is a new freedom and a new pluralism, and consequently this is a time of many doubts. The college experience itself is a course in criticism. The professor of English literature asks us to criticize poetry, the philosophy professor requests an evaluation of thought. The science teacher asks us to experiment, to work to a conclusion through trial and error. We are encouraged to question presuppositions in almost every field. The theology professor, however, may well suggest that this bag is closed with a tight knot. But this is a time, above all times, when a person must appropriate and interiorize faith, formulate his own personal and unique way of believing. To do this he must be allowed some marginal room for criticism and doubt, some testing, trial and error. The theology of memorized statements has to yield to a theology of questioning. Painful as it may be, each of us must ask himself if he really believes. Without posing the question, all answers will be meaningless.

It is a risky business, no doubt, and no one will feel the ponderous weight of risk more than the one who has the courage to carry it. Leaving the ordered security of the past is the only way to new growth, but it is like spending a night in a strange house. We sleep much better at home, where all the familiar objects, like the nightlamp and the bathroom, are in familiar places, where we can find them when needed. Our need for security wants to lean on the familiar. We feel threatened by the new precisely because it is unknown and untested. To take the structure of childhood faith and re-build it is like setting out to a new destination. We don't know what it will be like because growth is not prestructured for anyone. The road to firm and mature faith is strewn with many anxious moments, sudden feelings of agnosticism, a sharing in the loneliness of Jesus: "My God, my God, why have you forsaken me?" The mature believer is a search-ing believer. He will not settle for a familiar place in the sun, but will always be moving on to new heights.

Faith in adulthood: The crisis of meaning

The occupational hazard of being over thirty is the boredom of repetition. When all the days begin to look pretty much the same, and when the unrealis-tic dreams of youth have been cut down to size, the weariness of welldoing sets in. The mind asks tiredly: What's it all about? Life becomes luke-warm. There is nothing to unify life, to infuse it with meaning. Occasional "kicks" are only a dis-traction. You have to go back to being yourself, back to the galleys of drudging human existence.

The adult crisis of faith is to discover in one's relationship with God this meaning, a reason to live and a reason to die. Frankl's theory of logo-therapy suggests that meaning is the very bread of human life. The crisis of life after age thirty is to find meaning in life and to make sense of the universe. It is a time when we become too old to be young and are still too young to be old. This is the time of life when most breakdowns occur, when the incidence of alcoholism is highest, and most suicides are committed. The great psychiatrist, Carl Jung, once observed that most of his patients in middle life could "find no sense in living."

The basic problem is disillusion. All the romanticized dreams of youth are permanently frustrated, and the zest for struggle is dead. People tend to go forward while looking backward. After forty, the individual feels that he is "over the hill." He feels like an athlete on a losing team in the closing minutes of the game when it is too late to win, too late to be a hero. His mistakes and shortcomings have a malicious way of catching up with him. Psychiatrist Jung writes:

> They are depressed. They may ask themselves, "What next?" "Where am I going?" The inevitable answer must be death—and at least half of the journey has been completed. To the man or woman who only a short while before was planning big things, that answer is a shock, for where religion once served to make the last half of life a preparation for what was to come, such religious experience is missing in the lives of many people today.

> I am now convinced that I never had a case (in middle life) that did not originate in a spiritual unrest. . . . Almost a third of my cases are suffering from no clinically definable neurosis, but from the senselessness and emptiness of their lives. It seems to me, however, that this can well be described as the general neurosis of our time. . . . Among all my patients in the second half of life—that is to say, over thirty-five—there has not been one whose problem in the last resort was not that of finding a religious outlook on life. It is safe to say that everyone of them fell ill because he had lost that which the living religions of every age have given to their followers, and none of them has been really healed who did not regain his religious outlook.

> Our pursuit of scientific knowledge and the trend of our entire educational system has been a glorification of

intellect and a corresponding disintegration of the basic values which make intellect worth having. (From *Modern Man in Search of a Soul*)

It is not only those who are growing old, finding the shadows of life lengthening, who are in search of meaning; there is a desire in every human being to find some kind of unity and coherence, some meaning in the diverse experiences of life. All of us instinctively want to find some kind of key that will unlock the secret and meaning of good days and bad, joy and sorrow, youth and old age, sickness and health, life and death. We want some kind of a framework of understanding within which we can find perspective, and be freed from the delusion of confusing that which is truly important with the monumental trivia of life. It is, I think, only the overview of faith that can provide for us this insight into life, this meaning of life. As Dag Hammarskjold recalls in his book, *Markings,* "On the day I first really believed in God, for the first time life made sense to me and the world had meaning."

The vision of faith

The following is a suggested synthesis of faith-convictions. It is offered as a smorgasbord, from which you can choose the things that are meaningful to you, rather than as a definitive statement. Each of us must digest the truths seen through the eyes of faith in his own personal way. Like food, these truths will sustain us only to the extent that we have digested them, and have made them a part of ourselves. Our trust in these truths must be absolute. Otherwise, we will lose the very thing we need most: a perspective of life that will give us a reason to live and a reason to die. Without such perspective, life can seem only lonely and perplexing.

(1) *"God is Love"* (1 John 4:16). St. John defines God as being love. It means that all God ever does is love. His love, like all real love, is self-diffusive; it asks only to give, to share. Dietrich Bonhoeffer, in his *Ethics,* suggests that, in trying to understand John's definition of God, we must not take the word "love" as our starting point, but we must begin with the word "God." As St. John says, only he who knows God can know what love really is. "It is not," Bonhoeffer adds, "that we first of all by nature know what love is and therefore know also what God is." No one can know what God is, and therefore understand the meaning of love, unless God reveals himself to that man. No one can know what love really means unless he first knows God through the experience of faith.

St. John says that love originates in God (1 John 4:10) and that we perceive God's love in Jesus, especially in his act of dying for us (1 John 3:16). It is an "utterly unique event," according to Bonhoeffer, that God laid down his very life for us in Jesus. "God was in Christ," St. Paul writes, "reconciling the world to himself, not holding men's faults against them" (2 Corinthians 5:19). Jesus is, therefore, the living definition of love, and, as Bonhoeffer says, "the only definition of love." Love is what God unchangeably is, and Jesus is the revelation of what God is.

(2) *Gove loves us as we are.* The kind of love that brings us into the fullness of life is not the love which regards what we have been or what we might become, but the love which takes us as we are. And this is the way God loves us. Of course we are imperfect, but God sees us as beings in process. He takes us, at whatever point we may be in our development, as we are. The deadliest of all delusions about God is the notion that he can be

angry. It is an anthropomorphism and deception that we must bury beyond all possibility of resurrection. We must prayerfully meditate on God's unchanging nature. Theologians call it his "immutability." God is always the same. He can neither hurt nor be hurt. He is not subject to the heat and coldness, the ups and downs, the mercurial emotions that affect us. We must not make God to our image and likeness. This would be the death of all authentic faith.

Rudolph Bultmann in his *Theology of the New Testament*, writes that it would be fatally erroneous to think of the "wrath of God," to which the Bible refers, as an emotion of anger. God cannot be angry, because whatever God does, God is. Whatever is in God is eternally in God. The respected Anglican Biblical scholar, C. H. Dodd, in his work *The Epistle to the Romans,* warns that the "wrath of God" does not mean a feeling or attitude in God towards man, but "rather an effect in the realm of objective facts." This is to say, that we can separate ourselves from God if we choose to, but God who is unchangeable remains forever loving. The only change resulting from sin is in ourselves and in our world. It is this change in us and in our world that is metaphorically called the "wrath of God." This phrase does not refer to anything that is actually in God.

The reality of sin and separation from God is too clearly depicted in God's revelation, and in the message of Christ, to be denied. A man can lose his soul and forfeit his eternal happiness. Man is free, and he can freely walk away from love, even when love is opening its arms to receive him, even when it is opening its arms on a cross. However the reality of God's love is not at all diminished or compromised by this fact of human freedom. He is unchangeably love, and all that he does is love.

We might consider an analogy with the sun. The sun only shines, just as God only loves. It is the nature of the sun to shine, to offer warmth and light; it is the nature of God to love, to offer the warmth and light of union with himself. But we are free, as we know, to get out of the sun, to retreat from it into places where its warmth and brightness cannot reach us. We can put small barriers, like a parasol, between the sun and ourselves. We can also block the sun out completely, locking ourselves in darkened dungeons where the sun cannot reach us. But we do not change the sun simply because we have left its warmth and light. So it is with God, we can reject the light and warmth of his love; it is within the scope of our human freedom to do so. However, as the sun continues to shine, even after we have separated ourselves from its effects, so God continues to love, no matter what our choices are.

We have all hidden, in large ways or small, from his light and warmth. We have taken refuge in a series of distractions, concealed ourselves under the cover of pretext and delusion, but the sun of God continues to shine. He continues to love us, to offer the gifts that will bring our total fulfillment. There is no time in the history of a human life that one cannot go back into the light and warmth of God's love. No matter what obstacles sin and selfishness have erected, God is always there for us, always offering himself in warmth and light. It is important that we understand this during life. The only alternative would be to discover in death what we never knew in life, and with St. Augustine lament, "Too late, too late, O Lord, have I loved you. . . . Memory is indeed a sad privilege."

It is a sad alternative: to discover only in death what we never realized in life.

(3) *God's Providence rules the lives of man.* St. Paul, in speaking to the men of Athens, says:

> God, who made the world and everything in it, is the Lord of heaven and earth, and does not live in temples made by men. Nor does he need anything that men can supply by working for him, since it is he himself who gives life and breath and everything else to all men. . . . He himself fixed beforehand the exact times and the limits of the places where they would live. He did this so that they would look for him, and perhaps find him as they felt around for him. Yet God is actually not far from any one of us; as someone has said, "In him we live and move and have our being." (*Acts* 17:24-28)

Strictly speaking there is no such thing as time, as "before" or "after," in God. However, we are creatures of time, and in our limited way of understanding God, we must conceive his actions as temporal. And so we might say that, before God created this world, he knew all the possible worlds he could have created. In some of the possible worlds that God could have created, you and I existed; in others we did not. In some of the other worlds which God could have created, you and I would have had very different types of existence, different circumstances of life, different talents, different joys and sufferings.

However, in God's act of creation he was saying that he did not want these other worlds. He wanted this world. In his own eternal decree of creation, he wanted this blade of grass to spring through the earth at precisely the moment it did, and that leaf on the distant tree to fall at the precise moment when it will fall on a day in Autumn. He wanted you and me to be born of the parents who gave us life, at the precise moment he chose. He knew what we would look like, how we would sound, what we would be able to do and what we would not be able to do. He knew the agonies and ecstasies that life would ask of us and confer upon us. It was to this world that God said his "yes" of creation. Having seen the whole of our lives from all eternity, in the mystery of time God gives us these lives piece by piece, something like the pieces of a jig-saw puzzle which we must fit together. In putting together the pieces of this puzzle we must believe that he who has given us the pieces knows the beauty that will result when the final piece, the act of our dying, is put into place. St. Paul writes to the Romans: "We know that in all things God works for good with those who love him, those whom he has called according to his purpose."

God has, as it were, given us the lumber of our lives. Our response is to build, with whatever we have been given, a cathedral of praise. He has given us definite talents for a definite job which only we can do. There is no such word as "chance" in the vocabulary of God. He says to each of us what he said to his people of Israel: "And behold I am with you, and will keep you in all the places that you go, and will bring you again into this land. For I will not leave you until I have done what I have spoken of to you" (Genesis 28:13-15). Jesus requests his Apostles to repose all their trust in the fatherly providence of God:

> It is God who clothes the wild grass—grass that is here today, gone tomorrow, burned up in the oven. Won't he be all the more sure to clothe you? How little faith you have! Do not start worrying: "Where will my food come from? or my drink? or my clothes?" Your father in heaven knows that you need all these things. Instead, be concerned above everything else with his kingdom and with what he requires of you, and he will provide you with all these other things so do not worry about tomorrow. (Matthew 6:30-34)

173

It is the belief in God's Providence that puts us into contact with God in each moment of our lives, because each moment brings us into contact with his own divine and eternal plan for us. This recognition of faith infuses meaning into all the joys and all the sufferings of human existence as each of us knows it for his own.

(4) *Man's response to God: love of his fellow man.* It is a theological truism that we cannot give God anything directly. He already has everything. However, in the revelation of Jesus, we are clearly directed to place our response of love to God's love in the form of charity towards our neighbor. In fact, Jesus calls this love which we have for one another the badge of his discipleship: "A new commandment I give you; love one another. As I have loved you, so you must love one another. If you have love for one another, then all will know that you are my disciples" (*John* 13:34-35). All this is perhaps obvious to anyone who has read the New Testament carefully. What is not obvious, perhaps, is that the ability to love one another is God's gift to us. We do not win the favor of God by loving one another, but rather it is the favor of God that enables us to love one another.

St. John says: "We know that we have passed from death to life because we love our brothers. He who does not love abides in death" (*1 John* 3: 14). The whole first letter of St. John is a beautiful treatise on this marvelous but mysterious fact. In writing to the Corinthians, St. Paul tells them of the many gifts of God, and in the famous thirteenth chapter of *First Corinthians,* he describes the most excellent gift of God: charity. Finally, there is the description of the Last Judgment by Jesus. He portrays the saved coming into the blessedness of heaven:

Then the King will say to the people on his right, "You that are blessed by my father: come! come and receive the kingdom which has been prepared for you ever since the creation of the world. I was hungry and you fed me, thirsty and you gave me drink; I was a stranger and you received me into your homes, naked and you clothed me; I was sick and you took care of me, in prison and you visited me." . . . "I tell you, indeed, whenever you did this for one of the least important of these brothers of mine, you did it for me!" (*Matthew* 25:34-40)

(5) *God is our destiny.* Some years ago, after failing by several hundred yards to complete her swim across the English Channel, a woman named Florence Chadwick said that the reason for her failure was the morning fog which hung heavily above the Channel. She said: "If I could have seen the shore, I would have made it." The whole Christian view of life sees God as both the Alpha and Omega of human existence. We are, in this life and in this world, a pilgrim people on our way home. No synthesis of life, provided by the vision of faith, would be complete without a vision of the shore. In the mystery of the Transfiguration of Jesus, when the beauty of God momentarily flashed out of the person of Jesus, the reaction of Peter was typically human. He wanted to build three tents, to stay on that mountain forever.

It is typically human because all of us want to do this; we want to crystallize our moments of extreme happiness and remain within them forever. But our clocks and calendars continue their counting, and we must go down from these mountains of supreme happiness. However, if life and death are to have meaning for us, it is critical to remember that someday we shall ascend the mountain of God, and behold his beauty forever and ever. There will be a moment when all the clocks and calendars have finished their work for each of us. This is the Christian's sense of destiny. St. Paul writes to the Romans: "I consider that what we suffer at this present time cannot be compared at all with the glory that is going to be revealed to us." (*Romans* 8:18).

Conclusion

The overview of faith puts life into a meaningful perspective. It enables man to find a personalizing relationship with God in all the dimensions of human reality. Only the eyes of faith can see beneath the surface of things, and only the hope of faith gives a coherence to the disparate aspects of human existence. It deepens us not only in our unity with God but in our unity with one another. When we look at one another, the first thing we see is a body, an external appearance. But under the surface beauty or ugliness, in a deeper mode of existence is a person, a person with broken dreams and newborn hopes, a person of loneliness and love. And somehow, in an even deeper mode of existence, in the center of that person is God. The deepest mode of existence in all creation is the presence of God, whose being is shared by and mirrored in all creation. He is in the light in the sky, the suddenness of the storm, the first cry of the newborn baby, and in the last breath of the dying man. His pulse is the heartbeat of the universe.

In the vision of faith, God is found in joy, love, pain, and loneliness. There is nothing in all creation that is untouched by his presence. All the movements with which creation stirs reveal the life of a transcendent God deeply immanent in all things. He is present in the darkness of despair and in the light of hope. He is in laughter and in the cry of pain. He is in the high-noon and in the dead of night. There is no distant star, no drop of water at the bottom of the deepest ocean, no mountain or rock or fragile blade of grass that does not somehow share his life, and reveal his person.

To find God in all things requires the inner eyes of faith. Faith is the inner eyes that see him in the face of a child, in the first light of day, and in the darkness of night. Faith is the inner ears that hear God in the moaning of the wind, in the pounding of the surf against the shore, in the sing-sing voice of a child saying nursery rhymes, in the groaning of motors struggling up a hill, in the eruption of laughter, and in the labored breathing of those in pain. Faith is an inner set of hands that feels the touch of God in the crisp, whipping wind, in the soft trickle of rain, and in the pressure of another's hand in ours.

The life of faith is a life of search, but also a life of finding. It does not obliterate anything of natural reality. I do not love the rain only because God is in its wetness; I love the rain because it is rain. I do not love you only because God lies at the heart of you. I love you because you are you; it is only the recognition of your loveliness that leads me to the loveliness of God. I love a tree for its lumber and leaves, for the symmetry of its branches, for its prose and its poetry. It is only when I have loved a tree because it is a tree that I can find God who reposes veiled but available in all reality.

Life is not an aggregation of disparate things, unrelated and disconnected. All created reality is seen by the eyes of faith as arks of the covenant, tabernacles of God's presence and glory. All the diversity of creation finds unity in this vision, and all of reality is infused with the presence, power and glory of God, in whom all things live and move and have their being.

CHAPTER SEVEN

Getting To Know Jesus Christ

At that time Jesus said, "Father, Lord of heaven and earth! I thank you because you have shown to the unlearned what you have hidden from the wise and learned. Yes, Father, this was done by your own choice and pleasure. My Father has given me all things. No one knows the Son except the Father, and no one knows the Father except the Son, and those to whom the Son reveals him.

Come to me, all of you who are tired from carrying your heavy loads, and I will give you rest. Take my yoke and put it on you, and learn from me, because I am gentle and humble in spirit; and you will find rest. The yoke I will give you is easy, and the load I will put on you is light." (*Matthew* 11:23-28)

Knowing about Jesus and knowing Jesus

"Faith is God's work in man. . . . Only God can make a man a believer. . . . God takes and God keeps the initiative in the faith process. . . . Faith is totally God's gift." You will recognize these statements from the previous parts of this book. The other side of the coin is that man must freely accept the gift of God, correspond to his initiatives, cooperate with God's work in him. How do we do this? Are there any road map directions in God's word of revelation?

I am personally convinced that the answer is both in man's nature and in God's revealed word: Getting to know Jesus Christ. Notice that we are not being urged to know *about* Jesus, but to know *him*. As Cardinal Newman once said: "We do not build cathedrals to intellectual principles but to persons. It is only by persons that we are subdued, melted, won over." Faith is not something that must be intellectually understood as much as it is something that must be experienced and lived. It is a living relationship of love with God in, with, and through his Son, Jesus. St. John writes:

> This, then, is the witness (of God) about his Son: God has given us eternal life, and this life is in his Son. Whoever has the Son has this life; whoever does not have the Son of God does not have life. (1 John 5:11-12)

Jesus himself said: "I am come in order that men might have life, life in all its fullness (John 10:10). . . . I am the way, the truth, and the life; no one goes to the Father except through me (John 14:6). . . . When I am lifted up (on a cross), I will draw all men to myself (John 12:32). . . . Everyone whom my Father gives me will come to me. I will never turn away anyone who comes to me" (John 6:37). And Peter, preaching to his Jewish contemporaries, says of Jesus: "Salvation is to be found through him alone; for there is no one else in all the world, who has been given by God to men, by whom we can be saved" (Acts 4:12).

This, then, is the secret of faith and the genius of the believer: to cultivate a deep and warmly personal relationship with Jesus, so that everything one does becomes an act of love for and faithfulness to Jesus. Faith does not grow in biblical seminars or by constructing intellectual arguments for the plausibility of faith. Debating societies rarely produce lovers, saints, or heroes. Getting to know

Jesus and learning to love him faithfully is the heart of the matter.

Knowing and loving Jesus is not a simple matter. Knowing and loving are never simple. We are creatures of delusion, and, like the people of Israel in the course of their exodus to the promised land of God, we are tempted by idolatry. Knowing and loving demand choice and resolution. There is a detachment in every attachment, an emptying that precedes every filling, a death in every life. No man can serve two masters. And so we must be aware of our divided hearts, of the possibility that there are other forces at work in our lives which can make our faith-commitment anemic, half-hearted. There are idols, some beautiful and some ugly, which dilute our love and stifle our union with Jesus. Self-hatred as well as pride, puritanical prudishness as well as selfish overindulgence, fear and recklessness, adoration or detestation of one's mind or body; — are all idolatrous forms of self-preoccupation that turn our eyes inward and away from Jesus.

The answer to the many problems involved in a life of faith is always the same: Get to know Jesus. Do you have intellectual problems with faith? Don't get all lost in the distraction of abstract ideas. No one can reason his way into or out of faith. Get to know Christ Jesus. Abstract, theoretical problems about the origin and development of faith are usually dissolved in the actual experience. Experience always precedes understanding. Without the experience first, in any process of growth, we have nothing to reflect upon except abstractions and theories. Asking oneself or others about how faith could possibly come about is a blind alley. Such questions evaporate in the personal experience of the presence, power, and love of

Jesus. Get to know Jesus. All the mutterings of man about beauty aren't as beautiful as one violet. The only relevant book about faith will be written by believers sharing their experience of faith and giving their personal testimonials to grace.

Do you have a lot of problems with institutional religion? Most of us do. Liturgies often seem dull, sermons uninspiring, and heroes are not easy to come by. Many of us bear some scars from bad experiences. There is always some nasty nun or preachy priest in the personal history of each of us. An old, Irish ditty has it: "To live above with the Saints we love, ah, that is the purest glory; to live below with the saints we know, ah, that is another story." Sometimes the institutional Church seems to make being a card-carrying, almsgiving Christian more important than being a loyal and loving follower of Christ. Don't get detoured by the painful appearances of God's pilgrim people. Get to know Jesus Christ. He will help you to see that this weak people is really his people, and that he is among them.

Do the Mass and the Sacraments seem like stale rituals? Does the Bible sound more like bad than good news? Are you turned off? Get to know Jesus. He will help you to see that he is the celebrant of every Mass; he will help you to find life and meaning in the Bible. He really does have something to say to us in the Scriptures. In your experience of human weakness (welcome to the club!), don't be discouraged. In the sacrament of Penance, he will offer you understanding and forgiveness. But don't ever go into that confessional box except to meet him, to apologize to him, and to hear his words of forgiveness and understanding.

If the Mass, the Sacraments and prayer services of the institutional Church are not places of encounter with Jesus, the Lord, they are almost meaningless. But sometimes these exercises of faith seem stale to us; they do not seem to have much influence on us or our lives, precisely because we have not yet come to know Jesus. We may have gone to religious services out of a begrudging sense of duty, to avoid sin, or to win some favor from God; we should be going to encounter Jesus Christ.

Only he can help us see our lives and everything we do as a part of our relationship with him. As we come to know Jesus, the false dichotomy between faith and life will disappear. Our joys and sorrows, successes and failures, gains and losses will all be recognized as a part of God's loving plan, unfolding itself in our lives and in our world. This coming-alive in faith, this renewed vision of the meaning of ourselves, this achievement of identity in Christ is possible only through a living, loving relationship with Jesus. Viktor Frankl writes:

> A thought transfixed me: For the first time in my life I saw the truth as it is set into song by so many poets, proclaimed as the final wisdom by so many thinkers. The truth—that love is the ultimate and highest goal to which man can aspire. Then I grasped the meaning of the greatest secret that human poetry and human thought and belief have to impart: the salvation of man is through love and in love. (From *Man's Search for Meaning*)

The Jesus of the Gospels

Jesus began his public life at age thirty because he was a practicing rabbi, and no one was allowed to take up rabbinical practice before attaining this age. *Rabbi* was a term applied to the teachers of Judaism, which was the name given to the religion of the Jews after the Babylonian captivity, roughly about 500 B.C. In the 500 years before Jesus, Judaism had incorporated many innovations, such as new classes like the Scribes, new places of worship called synagogues in addition to the temple. But the main emphasis of Judaism fell on the letter of the law.

Somehow in the process of religious evolution, these laws had become so numerous that devout Jews were finding the yoke of Yahweh something of an albatross. Being an essentially religious people, the stigma of being outside the oppressive law carried with it not only moral but strong social sanctions. The "sinner" was an outcast of human society. There was little margin left for error, and an even smaller margin left for a rabbi who told the chief priests and elders of the people: "I tell you solemnly, tax collectors and prostitutes are making their way into the kingdom of God before you." (*Matthew* 21:31).

St. Luke tells us that the audiences of Jesus were composed mostly of tax collectors and sinners who wanted to hear him and be near him. The Pharisees, members of a sect within Judaism who insisted most vehemently on observance of the law, and the Scribes, the scholars, and intellectuals of Judaism, were complaining. "This man," they said, "welcomes sinners and even eats with them!" (*Luke* 15:3).

This was the crucial and divisive issue: How does God regard the sinner? All of us have a tendency to enlist God in the ranks of our own causes, and to sign his name as a subscriber to our opinions. The Scribes and Pharisees were no exception to this rather human tendency. They looked upon the sinner and human weakness rather darkly, and felt that there was nothing left for God to do but join them in their opinion. They could not understand how this young rabbi from Nazareth could possibly be so tolerant of weakness and so open-armed to sinners. They confronted his disciples, wanting to know how their master could be so compromising with human frailty.

> When Jesus heard this he replied, "It is not the healthy who need the doctor, but the sick. Go and learn the meaning of the words: 'What I want is mercy, not sacrifice.' I did not come to call the virtuous but sinners." (*Matthew* 9:11-13)

When his critics came face to face with Jesus, to confront him with their charge of excessive compassion for the weak, Jesus told them three parables. The first had to do with a lost sheep and a dutiful shepherd who searches out and takes into his arms his straying sheep. The second was that of a woman who loses a coin and sweeps her whole house and searches until she finds it. The third had to do with a young man who preferred to sow his wild oats in the big city rather than plant grain in his father's fields in the farm country. This last parable is no doubt familiar. There is something deeply touching about it, something that reaches right into the heart of God. I think that, if Jesus were telling the story today, he would tell it something like this:

> Once there was a man who lived with his two sons on a sizeable farm in the country. One day the younger of the two boys came to his father with a surprise announcement: "I've had it with the chickens and crickets. I'm cutting out for the big city and the big time. This place is nowheresville."

> The father pleaded with his son: "Are you really going to leave me? You know how much I want and need you here." But the younger son had little sympathy for his father's plea. "Aw come off it, Pops. Save the sermon, and just give me the cash. You've been saving a long time, and you were going to give me half, weren't you? Well I want my money while I'm in the prime of life. I'm going to live it up while I'm still young."

184

So the father reluctantly gave his son his inheritance and watched him leave. The father's heart was no doubt heavy with grief as his son, wallet bulging with his inheritance, walked away without even a backward look over his shoulder. But the hardest part was yet to come.

Stories came back from the city. "Hey, Mister," people returning from the city called out to him, "that's some son you've got. You must be real proud of him. It's strictly booze, broads, and bawdy songs." All his neighbors gave him that sad, knowing look that is hung like a wreath around the neck of "fathers who have failed."

Meanwhile, a famine strikes. Unemployment figures are up, higher than ever before. And the small-town boy with the big-time dreams soon comes to the end of his bankroll. All the freeloaders for whom he bought drinks so often and the floozies who welcomed him into their arms for a nominal sum don't seem to recognize the prodigal son or remember his name very well.

He staggers from one to the other, begging for a job. Anything. Someone half seriously offers him a job: "Tell you what, fella, I'll give you a job. You can feed the pigs on my farm. For your pay you can eat all the husks and swill you want. Just give the rest to the pigs. It ain't much, but it'll keep you alive. These are bad days, you know."

So he takes it. And what he can keep down keeps him alive, until once, while he's down on his knees at the pig trough, nostalgic thoughts of home sweep like a flood into his mind. He experiences a kind of contrition that is born of hunger. He decides to go home. And that night, while he lies in the field waiting for merciful sleep to come, he prepares an act of contrition, and memorizes it:

"Dad, I'm not worthy to ask you to take me back as a son. I really don't deserve it. But I was eating the husks and swill of hogs to stay alive. Then I remembered how you treat the hired hands on the farm, how you provide them with warm meals and soft beds. Dad, would you take me back as a hired hand on your farm?"

The first step is always the hardest for us humans, especially when it means I've been wrong! But starvation has a persuasive logic that has often driven men to the most desperate deeds. And so the boy starts on the long road back home.

It is twilight as he comes into sight. The father is sitting on the front porch, his eyes fixed hopefully on the road. The neighbors noticed that he was there every night since his son left home, always looking, always hoping, until darkness settled over the land, and he would finally take his heavy heart to bed. The human heart, someone once said, never really breaks; it just aches and aches and aches.

But this night it was to be different. The aging eyes that had filled so often with the tears of bitter memories, fixed as usual on the road from the city, see the figure of a man approaching. The eyes of the father now fill with a new kind of tear and his heart begins to pound with a new kind of hope. He can tell . . . it's his walk, the way he swings his arms . . . all the things that only love notices. He runs out to the road, and he gathers his son into his arms.

The boy begins his memorized act of contrition. But he doesn't even get to the part about being taken back as a hired hand. The father's firm arms embrace him warmly, and the son buries his tearful face against his father's neck. He can feel the sobs of joy in his father's chest; he can feel his father's tears running down onto his own face.

Then he hears his father's voice: "Quick, get a good suit out for my son. I don't want him in these rags. Get out the best of everything for him. Slaughter the best calf we've got and begin roasting it. And someone get musicians in here. We are going to have the biggest party this valley has ever seen. My son is home! My son is home again! It's as though he had died, but has come back to life again."

The little farmhouse is soon alive with the aroma of roasted calf and the sounds of celebration, when the older son comes in from the field after a hard day's work. He meets one of the hired hands down at the well, and he asks: "Hey, what gives?" His face and heart turn to steel when he hears the answer: "The kid came home tonight." "My brother?" he asks. "You've got it, your little brother," the hired hand says cynically.

"Listen, you go in there and tell my father that I'll never put another foot inside that house as long as that kid is there."

When the father gets the message of his older son, he comes out and goes down to the well. "What is it, Son?"

"What is is? I'll tell you what it is. Look at this face. Remember me? I'm the one who stayed here. Look at these hands. See those callosses? That's from work, hard work on this farm. They're the hands that worked twice as hard when he went away. I was there that night. Remember? I heard him tell you how out of date you are, how fed up he was with everything you are and stand for. I was here when the stories came back from the city and broke your heart. I heard you sobbing half way through the night, and I have learned to hate my brother with everything in me. Now he comes home, and you give him a great big party. There's no fool like an old fool. You never gave a party like this for me and my friends. I never got a party. And I'm the one who stayed here."

The father then puts his arm over the shoulder of his older son, and gently moves him in the direction of the farmhouse. "Son, you're right. You deserve a party for your faithfulness, and you can have one anytime you want it. Everything I have is yours.

"I understand how you feel, but there's something I would like you to try to understand: what goes on in the heart of a father when his child who was lost comes home to him. Try to understand how a father feels when his child who was dead has come back to life again." (Adapted from *Luke* 15:11-31)

The story of Jesus was perfect, a perfect answer to the question about God's attitude towards human weakness that had been forced on him. "This," Jesus said, "is how my father regards sinners." The Scribes and Pharisees apparently did not understand. And sometimes I wonder whether you and I fully understand. Sometimes I think that we really do not understand Jesus because we insist on painting frowns on the face of God. We are distrustful of God's understanding and tenderness. When God takes us back into his love, as the father in the parable took his own son into his arms, there is something in us that wants to ask: "What's the catch?" It is so difficult for us who are unloving to know a God who is love.

The theory in practice:
Jesus deals with sinners

The whole life of Jesus is a living confirmation of this parable. "Love one another as I have loved you" derives its meaning only from the life of Jesus. No one was ever turned away or rejected because of weakness. He seems to understand and accept the human condition of frailty much better than you or I can.

The Prostitute (Luke 7:36-50): On an occasion, when Jesus was dining with a Pharisee named Simon, a very strange episode interrupted the meal. A woman entered the room. The presence of women was not permitted at such banquets. But she was not only a woman; she was one of the local prostitutes. The Roman liturgy identifies this woman with Mary Magdalen. The prostitute flings herself at the feet of Jesus, and her warm tears bathe his feet. She wipes them with her hair, and anoints them with a fragrant balm. Simon, being an exacting Pharisee with little compassion for human weakness, is beside himself with self-righteous indignation. So Jesus asks him the question about who loves more, the one who has been forgiven more or the one who has been forgiven less. When Simon gives the obvious answer. Jesus tells him quite plainly:

> "Simon," Jesus said, "you see this woman? I came into your house, and you poured no water over my feet, but she has poured out her tears over my feet and wiped them away with her hair. You gave me no kiss of greeting, but she has been covering my feet with kisses ever since she came in. You did not anoint my head with oil, but she has anointed my feet with balm. For this reason

I tell you that her sins, her many sins, must have been forgiven her or she would not have shown such great love. It is the man who is forgiven little who shows little love." Then Jesus said to her, "Your sins are forgiven." Those who were with him at table began to say to themselves, "Who is this man, that he even forgives sin?" But Jesus said to the woman, "Your faith has saved you; go in peace."

It seems to be true that God's grace and forgiveness had already cleansed this woman of guilt before Jesus confirmed it with his own assurance. Notice that he says that her sins must have already been forgiven because she is capable of great love. This underlines the truth we have already discussed, that, when someone knows God, he will know how to love. When God touches a man with his grace, that man is transformed, and the sign of his transformation is a new ability to love. And this is the way it is with all of us: genuine love of God and our neighbor arises from the recognition of our sinfulness and need for God, which is the condition for receiving the healing touch of God. Self-righteousness is incompatible with love. We do ourselves great harm when we try to rationalize and justify our weakness. Simple admission of our human condition is a necessary step towards God's forgiveness and mercy.

If the Roman liturgy is right in identifying this woman with Mary Magdalen, what a testimonial to the forgiving love of Jesus she became! It was Mary who stood at the foot of Christ's cross, remembering perhaps that he had once consoled and defended her when she was a woman of public shame. We can well imagine that she must have been the object of taunting remarks as she stood there on the hill of Calvary. "Hey, look who's here. . . . It's Mary the whore! Don't forget, baby, we knew you when. Who are you trying to kid with all this pious stuff?" But the woman who had seven devils cast out of her was equal to all this. People who really love God are strangely deaf to the taunts of those who do not understand. They seem to believe that we are worth only what we are worth in the eyes of God. They know what it is to be free, really free.

Love isn't very good at calculating difficulties or dangers to self. And so, while the Apostles huddled in fear, locked in the upper room, from Good Friday through Easter Sunday, it was the prostitute whom Jesus had loved into greatness that was out on the road. It was she who was commissioned to bring the word of his resurrection to the others. It was she who was the first to know that he had risen. It was she of whom Jesus said: "Wherever the story of my life will be told, the story of this woman's love for me will be told." It is she who stands as a living reminder of the transforming power of Jesus and his love. As Steinbeck once mused: "All the sins of men are only attempted shortcuts to love." Once this woman had found the real thing in Jesus, the shortcuts were buried in her past and in his mercy.

The Adulteress (*John* 8:3-11): Those jealous guardians of legality, the Scribes and Pharisees, were forever trying to force Jesus into a dilemma over the observance of the law. After all, they reasoned, this was the function and expertise of rabbis. They were in charge of the interpretation and sanction of the law. You will recall many of their attempts to make Jesus give up his emphasis on love and mercy; they felt he was neglecting his rabbinical duty.

The technical problem that was forced on Jesus in the case of the woman taken in adultery is something like the one which the Pharisees had brought to him about Caesar's coin. If Jesus authorized the death of the adulteress, he would be violating Roman law, which did not permit the Jews to administer capital punishment. If, however, he were to recommend mercy he would be violating the Mosaic law. As with the question of the coin of the realm, Jesus put the burden back on his questioners.

> They asked him this as a test, looking for something to use against him. But Jesus knelt down and started writing on the ground with his finger. As they persisted with their question, he looked up and said, "If there is one of you who has not sinned, let him be the first to throw a stone at her. Then he bent down and wrote on the ground again. When they heard this they went away one by one, beginning with the eldest, until Jesus was left alone with the woman, who remained standing there. Jesus looked up and said, "Woman, where are they? Has no one condemned you?" "No one, Sir," she replied. "Neither do I condemn you," said Jesus, "go home now and sin no more."

St. Augustine, in his commentary on the *Gospel of St. John,* says simply that, after the Scribes and Pharisees had slunk away, ". . . there were left only two: human misery and divine mercy." It is a good summary, not only of this episode in the life of Jesus, but in some larger sense it is a summary of the meeting of every one of us with Jesus.

Dismas, the Good Thief (Luke 23:39-43): St. Luke tells us that one of the two criminals crucified with Jesus began to challenge him: "Aren't you supposed to be the Christ? Save yourself and us, too!" The other thief tried to silence him: "Have you no fear of God at all? We are getting a punishment that we deserve. We are paying for what we did. But this man has done nothing wrong." Then, perhaps, raising his eyes to the plaque above the head of Jesus, which indicated the "crime" for which he was dying, Dismas read: "This is Jesus of Nazareth, the King of the Jews." The plaque was part of the ceremonial of crucifixion, so that by-standers and passersby would know the reason for the punishment. Death by crucifixion was usually a lingering form of dying, usually lasting two or three days. We remember that Pontius Pilate was surprised that Jesus had died in a matter of two or three hours.

Then the man we call Dismas said his prayers, perhaps the only sincere prayer he had ever said in his entire life:

> "Jesus . . . when you come into your kingdom, will you please remember me?" And Jesus, turning to him, replied: "You can be sure of this. Today you will be with me in paradise."

Jesus, as always, even in the agony of his own dying, was the "man for others." His words to the dying Dismas were the last that he said to any man before his own death. But his mercy is the same, yesterday, today, and always. There can be no question that this gift of love and mercy has been repeated uncountable times down the long course of human history and human weakness.

The Twelve Apostles: Like any other rabbi and itinerant preacher of his times, Jesus chose a small group of twelve men, whom he invited to be his constant companions and preachers of his gospel (*Mark* 3:14). All of these men, except Judas Iscariot, are now canonized for our admiration and imitation. But, in all honesty, they were not "born saints." In fact, when Jesus first called them, they were a rather strange assortment of human misery. They are classic examples of men who were loved into greatness by the patience of Jesus. All greatness, it would seem, is somehow born of patient love; and these men were no exceptions. They were all rather slow learners. They found an egocentric prudence the better part of valor, when their own safety was threatened; they were cowards. Their number included a loudmouth, two mama's boys, a bullhead, and an apparent birdbrain. They were just as weak as you and I can be.

The central figure among them was Simon, son of Jonah, known as the Rock. In fact, this man wasn't very much of a rock at all; he was more like a sandpile of human weakness. His first question, upon being invited into the discipleship of Jesus, was: "What's in it for me?" And after three years in the service of Jesus, when the Lord told the Apostles of his coming passion and death, it was the loudmouth Peter who protested that this wasn't a very good idea. Jesus had to tell him the plain truth: "The way you think is not God's way of thinking, but man's" (*Matthew* 16:21-23).

At the Last Supper this same Peter arrogantly denied the prediction of Jesus that Peter would disown him. He suggested that maybe one of the others might be so weak, but never the Rock. Of course, he did disown Jesus. While Jesus was being tried for his life before the Jewish court of the Sanhedrin, Peter waited anonymously in the courtyard outside, posing as a disinterested bystander. When he was recognized as a companion of Jesus, the Rock not only denied any knowledge of Jesus, but even swore an oath before God that he did not know Jesus at all. As Jesus was being led out of the palace of the High Priest on his way to prison and death, Peter was there in the courtyard bellowing his frightened denials of Jesus.

> . . . and the Lord turned and looked straight at Peter, and Peter remembered what the Lord had said to him, "Before the cock crows today, you will have disowned me three times." And Peter went off in the darkness and cried his heart out. (*Luke* 22:61-62)

On the next morning, Good Friday, when Jesus was bound and led as "the Lamb of God" before the Roman governor, Pontius Pilate, who alone could pronounce the sentence of death by crucifixion, the Apostles went into hiding. When Jesus really needed them, they let him down. There is no evidence of their presence (except for John) during the last agony of Jesus at the hands of his people. Their commitment to Jesus had deserted their memories and their hearts. So Jesus died alone.

On Easter Sunday, the morning of his resurrection, the Apostles were still in hiding, behind locked doors, with baited breath and chattering teeth. They feared that, if the Jews wanted to rip out all memory of Christ by the roots, they too might have to suffer and die. In the face of this possibility they had no wish to stand up and be counted for Christ. So they bolted the doors of the Upper Room, prisoners of their own fears.

It might be well, even if all other words of Jesus wash out of our memories, to recall his first words as he came in his risen glory into that Upper Room. The Apostles did not wish to share his pain and death, but he wished to share his triumph and glory with them. When Jesus confronted his tense and frightened Apostles, he did not berate them for their cowardice and unfaithfulness. He didn't ask Peter to stand up and repeat his exchange with the crowd in the courtyard of the High Priest. He didn't even ask them why the door was bolted. He simply entered and said:

"Shalom. Be at peace." (*Luke* 24:36)

It might be well for all of us, who insist on imposing limits on the patience and understanding of Jesus to remember the tenderness of his greeting. Like Peter, there is something in us that wants to say: "Depart from me, Lord. I am a sinful man." But he always says the same: "Shalom. Be at peace. I undertsand." When the Apostles see Jesus, they seem to have forgotten all he said about his resurrection. They think they are seeing a ghost, victims of mass hallucination. So the gracious Jesus offers them visual and tactile reassurance: "Look at my hands and feet. Yes, it is I. Touch me and see for yourselves. A ghost doesn't have flesh and bones, as you see I have." (*Luke* 24:39-40). When they remain numb, even after these words, he offers them a further reassurance of the reality of his resurrection by asking for and eating a piece of grilled fish and some honeycomb.

"Shalom. . . . Be at peace. . . . I understand," is the constant word of Jesus to the Apostles and to us. Peace in all the storms of life. Peace when your heart is sinking at failure. Peace when your world seems to be falling in on you. Peace in the monotony and endlessness of small things. Peace in the watching and waiting, when your heart is anxious and your hands are useless to do anything. But most of all, peace with your human weakness, when you can't seem to do anything right. "Shalom. I understand."

> "Do not let your hearts be troubled. Trust in God always, and trust in me. . . . Peace I leave you, my own peace I give you, a peace that the world cannot give. This is my gift to you, my peace." (*John* 14:1,27)

This is the Jesus that you and I must get to know. We must open our lives and our hearts to his person and his love. But we have doubts, don't we? We wonder if Jesus is real, and, if he is real, is he really available for us. Is he really there? We wonder if he will be to us what he was to the Apostles. Will we really experience peace and meaning if we invite him into our hearts and lives? Is his yoke really sweet and his burden light? Will he really refresh us when we are troubled and burdened?

Our struggle with doubts is reminiscent of a dark night when the Apostles were out on the Sea of Galilee.

> When evening came, Jesus was there alone, while the boat, by now far out on the lake, was battling with a heavy sea, for there was a head-wind. . . . When the disciples saw him walking on the water, they were terrified. "It is a ghost," they said, and cried out in fear. But at once Jesus called out to them saying: "Courage! It is I. Do not be afraid." It was Peter who answered: "Lord," he called out, "if it is you, tell me to come to you across the water."
>
> "Come to me!" said Jesus. (*Matthew* 14:23-29)

Maybe this is the heart and guts of faith. Maybe we have to be out in a boat, battling the heavy sea of life. Maybe we have to peer out into the mist to see his figure, a figure of mastery and hope that walks on the distant waters.

> And Jesus was a sailor
>   when he walked upon the water;
> And He spent a long time watching
>   from a lonely wooden tower.
> And just when He knew for certain
>   only drowning men could see Him,
> He said:
>   "All men shall be sailors, then,
>   until the sea shall free them . . ."
>
> (Leonard Cohen, from *Suzanne*)

Maybe we have to be filled with a million memories of the human lives that have been touched and transformed by his healing hands, of all the mortal misery that has been redeemed by his mercy.

But Jesus could be a ghost, a delusion. Maybe we have been brainwashed. Maybe the Gospels are only fiction. Freud claims that faith is an invention of the subconscious. There are many intelligent atheists. That figure of mastery and mercy, out there in the distance, over the sea, may be a mirage born of insecurity. How can I be sure?

> "Lord Jesus, if it is really you, tell me to come to you. Tell me to step out in faith across the waters of my life."
>
> "Come. Come to me!" says Jesus.

Other books by John Powell

A Reason to Live! A Reason to Die!
Teacher Manual
Valuable suggestions on how to use this book as a text on the psychology and theology of Faith in God.

919   $3.95

Why Am I Afraid to Tell You Who I Am?
Contemporary insights on self-awareness, personal growth and interpersonal communication.

B119 paperback $2.25

He Touched Me
This spiritual journey of the author's experience with prayer is a warm and inspirational sharing to help further the dialogue of prayer.

945 paperback $2.25

Why Am I Afraid to Love?
The capacity to love is within all of us. John Powell's perceptive and candid style makes it possible to release that power.

B106 paperback $1.95

The Secret of Staying in Love
John Powell takes the reader beyond *Why Am I Afraid to Tell You Who I Am?* into practical approaches for honestly communicating and sharing one's deepest emotions and feelings. This is the only level of communication that conveys the true me.

947 paperback $2.50